INTO THE CAGE

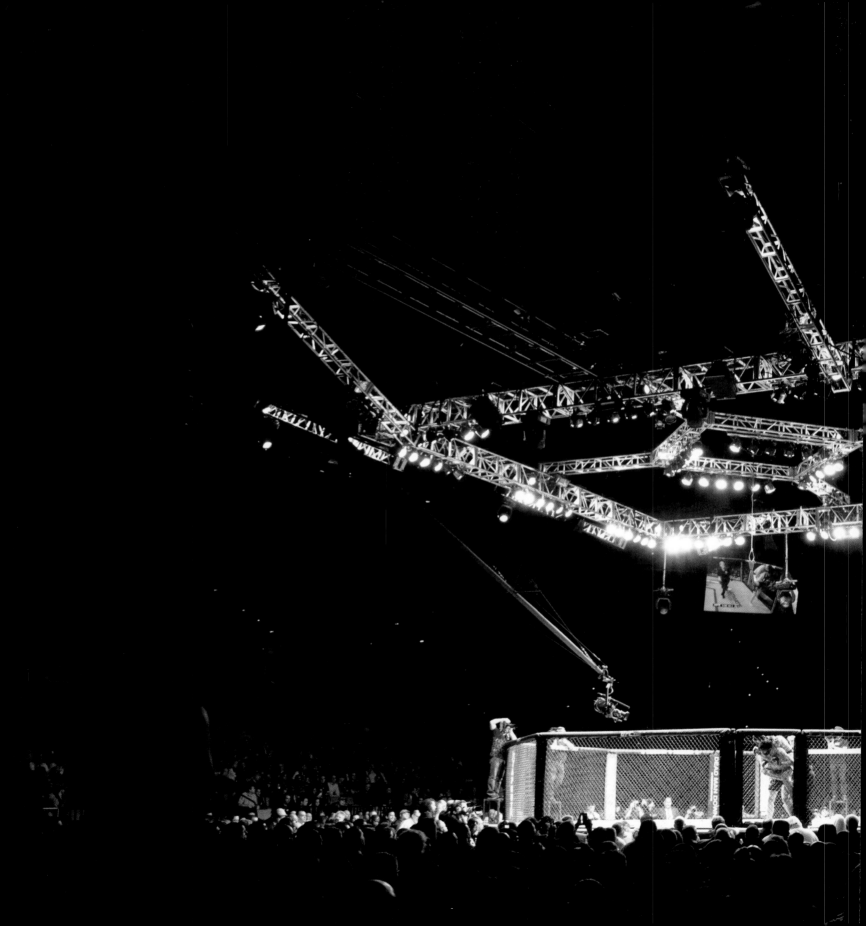

INTO THE CAGE

THE RISE OF UFC NATION

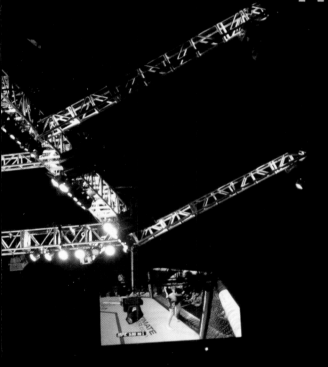

NICK GULLO

FOREWORD BY DANA WHITE

FENN
M&S

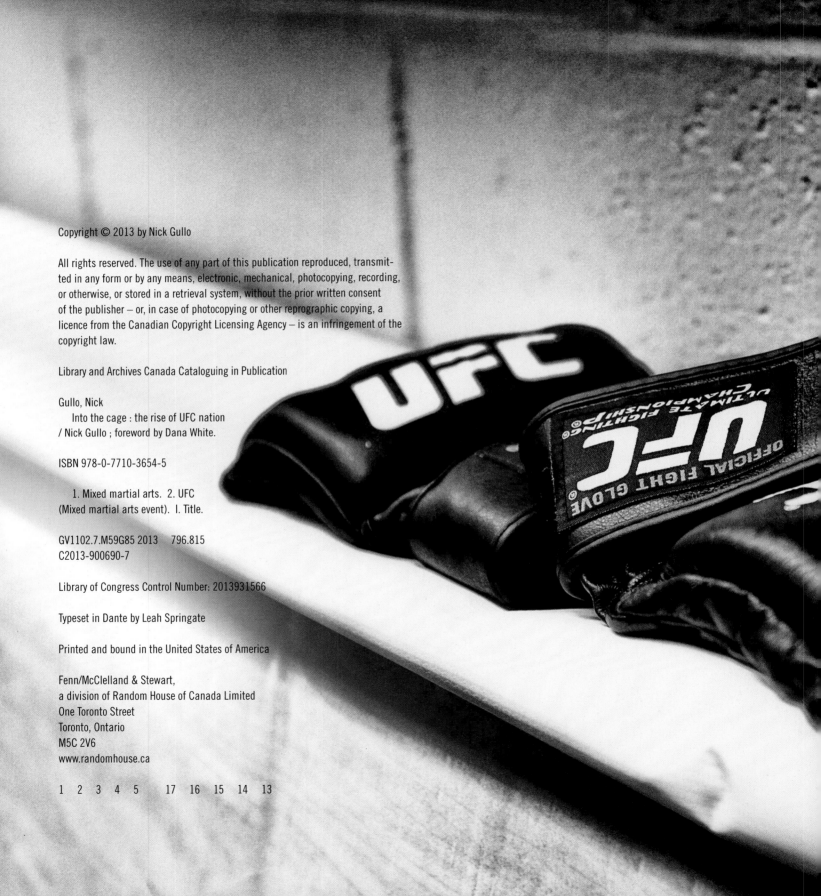

Library and Archives Canada Cataloguing in Publication

Gullo, Nick
    Into the cage : the rise of UFC nation
/ Nick Gullo ; foreword by Dana White.

ISBN 978-0-7710-3654-5

    1. Mixed martial arts. 2. UFC
(Mixed martial arts event). I. Title.

GV1102.7.M59G85 2013   796.815
C2013-900690-7

Library of Congress Control Number: 2013931566

Typeset in Dante by Leah Springate

Printed and bound in the United States of America

Fenn/McClelland & Stewart,
a division of Random House of Canada Limited
One Toronto Street
Toronto, Ontario
M5C 2V6
www.randomhouse.ca

1 2 3 4 5   17 16 15 14 13

CONTENTS

Foreword by Dana White ix

1   How Did This Happen? 1

2   The History of Mixed Martial Arts 9

3   Martial Arts Styles 27

4   The Hero's Journey 63

5   Fight Club 83

6   Do the Evolution 97

7   The Mountain 113

8   Heavy Is the Crown 131

9   Women's MMA 145

10 *The Ultimate Fighter (TUF)* 161

11 The Machine 173

12 Joe Rogan 187

13 Dana White 197

14 Fight Week 213

Photographic Captions and Credits 229

Acknowledgments 230

INTO THE CAGE

This year marks the twentieth anniversary of the UFC. It's been thirteen years since we bought the company, and despite all the progress, I never look back and pat myself on the shoulder. Maybe that's why we're successful. Lorenzo, Frank, and I know there is so much left to accomplish. That's what we focus on.

However, when I read this slice of UFC history, and flip through the photos, I'm grateful for the fighters and fans who have helped us propel MMA into the fastest-growing sport in the world.

Nick is one of my closest friends. With his unprecedented access he's crafted something truly unique. As he emphasizes throughout this book, the fighter's journey is a metaphor for life. We all start at the bottom. We all face adversity. But when we bow our heads and work through the hardships, refuse to surrender despite our doubts, we grow stronger. And growing stronger, we prevail. That's the journey of a champion.

Enjoy.

Dana White
UFC President

1: HOW DID THIS HAPPEN?

IT STARTED WITH A WHISPER. More than ever I'm convinced it *always* starts with a whisper . . .

Walking down the corridor, I hear music echoing through the walls, the crowd chanting, announcers hyping the main card—but this isn't how or when it started. This is 2008, which is somewhat of a way station in this tale, and where we are is inside a concrete tunnel beneath the MGM Grand Garden Arena in Las Vegas. Cramped quarters. Fluorescent gray light distorts shadows. A metal duct overhead spews cold air, but it's no comfort. I'm sweating, nervous. Dana White turns and flashes that iconic grin, and for a moment it's like old times—like we're teenagers again, ready to knock heads. "You cool?" he says.

I shrug, trying to play it off, like what waits beyond this tunnel is nothing, just a midday stroll through an empty stadium. Never mind the twelve thousand rabid fans.

No. I'm anything *but* cool. My stomach's rumbling and I've got this taste on my tongue, like I downed a glass of questionable milk and next I'll vomit in that passing can. But, like, pull it together, *dude,* because they—the PR lady to my left, the assistant holding a clipboard and a walkie-talkie, the camera guy—are all staring, and I know they're thinking, *Who is this guy? If they're such good friends, where the fuck has he been?*

And yeah, they're right to question. It's been eight years since Dana and I last saw each other.

Eight. Years.

Flip back through the calendar and that lands us pre-millennium. Since then, the world's endured hanging chads, planes careening into towers, green missile flares over Iraq, a foreclosure crisis. The last time Dana and I were together was on a return flight to Vegas. Here's the scene unfolding: I'm munching pretzels while Dana flips through a mixed martial arts (MMA) magazine. After some turbulence he leans in and whispers something. What's that? Oh,

he's mumbling about MMA, how it could be *the next thing*. Clouds pass outside the window and I'm hardly listening. I've got pressing concerns, like should I move my young family to the Gulf Coast, swap the Vegas desert for Florida's sandy beaches, abandon friends, and—

"I'm telling you, bro, this could be big," he says.

I glance at the article and give him a curt nod, but I know this won't appease him. Once Dana gets something in his head—whether it's a new "system" for beating the roulette wheel, a hot parlay for Sunday's games, or a guy who crossed him—forget it, you might as well toe the line. "Looks great," I say and turn back to the window.

"I'm fucking serious," he says.

"Yeah, all right, I heard you—*huge*. It could be huge."

"Asshole."

Okay. This clearly wasn't going to end. "What do you mean?" I say. "Like kickboxing? Or those strong-man competitions where they drag logs through the mud?"

"No, dipshit, a cage, they fight in a cage."

"Ohhh, tough-guy matches—didn't Mr. T win one of those?"

"You're a gorilla."

Of course in hindsight, I'm the idiot. Hurl the black roses, I'll gather them all. In retrospect, this exchange is akin to Moses preaching from the mount while some fool snickers and polishes the golden calf. But understand, Dana and I were friends, and what did he know about MMA? Back then he was teaching casino executives and their wives to sidestep and throw jabs, paying the family bills as a boxing coach. Yeah, on the side he managed Tito Ortiz, a cage fighter, so there was at least a tacit connection with this new obsession—but still, to my ears, the phrase *MMA* elicited two events: first, the legendary 1976 Muhammad Ali versus Antonio Inoki bout, wherein the champ flew to Japan and fought under hybrid rules that allowed kicking but no grappling, jabbing but no flying knees, and resulted in an absolute farce, with Inoki on his back much of the fight, throwing heels and flailing like a tempestuous child, for which Ali suffered blood clots in his

Liz Carmouche, first challenger to the UFC women's bantamweight belt, *UFC 157*.

leg that threatened amputation and hobbled him for the rest of his career; and second, in 1993, the first *Ultimate Fighting Championship* (UFC) on pay-per-view (PPV).

Everyone I knew tuned in to this inaugural UFC event, all of us frothing at the prospect of various disciplines clashing in the ring: kung fu versus boxing versus Krav Maga versus sambo. Mind you, these were the heady days of *Mortal Kombat* and *Virtua Fighter*, the arcades packed with kids—no, not just kids, also grown men—battling as Kung Lao, Liu Kang, and Kage-Maru. So after forking over fifty dollars for the PPV, we expected blitzkrieg action. Bruce Lee scissor kicks. Multi-hit combos. *Fatalities!*

Instead, we endured two hours of mismatched fighters, untrained camerawork, and hairband synth music. Yeah, there were some exciting moments, and yeah, Royce Gracie's Brazilian jiu-jitsu was impeccable, and yeah, he dominated all comers, and yeah, yeah, yeah, the core fans mythologize that first event and swear it was the greatest thing since Hagler versus Hearns—but to my untrained eyes all that mat work was akin to a typical high school wrestling match . . . *and I was a lifelong wrestler!*

Now, I know to some, the most devoted, this screams of heresy, but watch those early events and you'll see that the production value is just a notch above early 1980s Betamax porn. Scan the replays and note Art Jimmerson feinting with a single boxing glove during his bout with Gracie, which lasted all of two minutes before Gracie wrestled the hapless boxer to the ground and submitted him. This is a prime example of a bout that elicited pre-bell whoops and whistles and post-bell groans.

And check out the morbidly obese Teila Tuli sumo-charging across the ring at karate / savate champion Gerard Gordeau: Gordeau casually steps aside, Tuli crashes into the cage, falls to his knees, receives a kick in the face, and his tooth flies to the mat. At twenty-six seconds, the referee steps in, waving his hands. Now, while that was humorous, can you imagine such a hokey matchup today? And the good fights? Well, most of us didn't know how to watch them.

Here's Ken Shamrock summarizing one of his *UFC 1* victories as a shootfighter / wrestler, which came at just 1:49 after the opening bell: "I was fighting Patrick Smith. He's 250–0 in bare-knuckle fights. He's undefeated. I remember the bell rings, I go in there, and Patrick throws a hard kick. I shoot on him. I take him down. I punch him a few times. I drop back down to a heel hook. I crank his heel, I break his leg. AGHHHHH! The crowd booed. They were mad. No one understood what submissions were! They were like, 'What was that?' Even the announcers were like, 'He got him in, uh, some, uh, foot lock, or something . . . ' It was like no one knew. They didn't have an idea. Royce Gracie and myself were the only ones that really knew what submissions were, knew how to do submissions effectively in a real fight."

I think I'm on safe ground asserting that jiu-jitsu, like wrestling or judo, requires the audience to possess at least a basic understanding of the subtle strategies at work; and unfortunately, many of us watching that first event expected everything *but* fighters rolling across the mat for extended periods. And once they were down, we certainly didn't grasp what was happening.

So, no, I didn't imagine the sport growing into anything beyond its back-room status, much less *huge*.

—

Fast-forward five years from that plane flight: I'm in Florida, working, surfing, raising our daughter—only there's no cable television in the house (as in no CNN, no sports, no pay events, no reality TV. Nothing.) How such a thing happens is that the wife finds your young daughter lifeless in front of the television again and again, eyes glazed and thumb on the remote, and being an overprotective mother she pulls the plug and allows only DVDs through the front door. (To be fair, there was reason to worry. Once during dinner I spilled red wine on the rug and while my wife fretted with a spray bottle and towel, from nowhere our daughter blurted, "Oh,

Mommy, don't worry about that stain. You can Zap it out! Zap removes coffee, wine, cherries, even blood!")

So yeah, choosing my battles I conceded to the crackdown, which meant I'm not just across the country, I'm on a veritable desert island. But I heard things. Such as Dana whispering that mantra to Lorenzo Fertitta, another high school friend: "I'm telling you, bro, this thing could be big . . ."

Only Lorenzo listened, and with his older brother, Frank, they purchased the ailing UFC and installed Dana as president in 2001. But that's it. No clue how it was doing. Occasionally I received a Dana email exhorting me to visit, but I was slammed with life and work and just never found time to venture from the shore. That is, until the monstrous hand of God, in the form of Hurricane Katrina, swept through the Gulf of Mexico in 2005 and mangled the entire coast.

Cataclysm doesn't even begin to describe such an event, not at your doorstep.

We interpreted the signs, packed our vintage Airstream, and drove away from the debris, touring the country and eventually winding our way back West. Once in Vegas, I surprised my old friend with a phone call. He picked me up in a black Range Rover. I rubbed his bald head and hugged him. "It's been a long time, Gorilla," he said.

"I can't believe it," I said. "Tell me everything."

—

Now, nearing the black curtain at the mouth of the tunnel, the floor thumps with every step, but how it feels is like I just swallowed the red pill and that's why I've got these cold sweats. Welcome to the real. One moment I'm on the plane with my bro, close my eyes, and now—

Security guards surround us. A hand drops on my shoulder and passes me a laminated badge, *UFC 84: Penn vs. Sherk.* I stare at the flimsy rectangle and try to tune out the screeching walkie-talkies.

"You cool?" Dana again asks.

I grip the badge like a talisman and smile back. "I'm cool."

"Let's go." The drapes swing wide and we're rushed into darkness, shoved into limbs, bodies, bodies everywhere. Security clears a rough path. We round a barricade and a spotlight ignites. The crowd erupts. Cameras flash and I'm feeling my way . . . finally the splotches clear, and oh shit, he's gone. Swallowed whole. I'm knocked into a gate. Massive LCD monitors hang from the ceiling, and wait, there's Dana floating overhead, that bald head bigger than I could ever imagine.

It's too much. I let him go, knowing we'll catch up at the press conference. Chuckling to myself, I remember us drinking beer and slam-dancing to punk music in his bedroom—and what I wonder, what I can't fathom, is not how such a ridiculous idea inspired a whisper, but how a whisper grows so fucking deafening.

The facts. Trawling the web yields some neat-ish stats: MMA is the fastest-growing sport in the world (according to Simmons Research Database, gate attendance at UFC events from 2001 to 2008 increased more than 500 percent. Further, between 2005 and 2008, the fan bases of the NFL, NBA, MLB, MLS, and NASCAR each declined, while the UFC fan base increased more than 30 percent); UFC bouts typically draw 12,000 to 15,000 attendees and, according to third-party guestimates, upwards of 1.6 million PPV buys; *The Ultimate Fighter* reality TV series often attracts more than 1 million eyeballs; fights are broadcast in more than 145 countries and territories, and the UFC boasts 31 million fans in the United States and 65 million worldwide; hundreds of MMA companies, responsible for thousands of jobs, attend the UFC Fan expo twice a year; the *UFC Undisputed 2009* video game sold more than 3.5 million copies upon its release; UFC Octagon girl Arianny Celeste has graced the pages of *Playboy, Maxim, FHM,* and *The Atlantic*; most major news outlets cover MMA, with staff journalists cranking out the who/what/when/where/why of every MMA murmur and happening—

But enough already, as this is neither a MMA encyclopedia nor a Dana White biography—there's plenty enough compendiums and sites devoted to individual fighter stats, and as far as a bio, though I've injected plenty of D.W. anecdotes and history throughout this book, his bio is another project. So what you're holding here is my attempt to chronicle, and I hope make sense of, the maelstrom that he, Lorenzo, and Frank unleashed on our post-millennium world.

Some nights, usually after a stiff glass, I hear that whisper. So I break out the album and sift through old photos. Fuck yeah, I find it strange. Then, now. There, here. And in those moments, what I want more than anything is to raise my drink and for real swallow the red pill, just to see how deep this rabbit hole goes.

Before the fight.

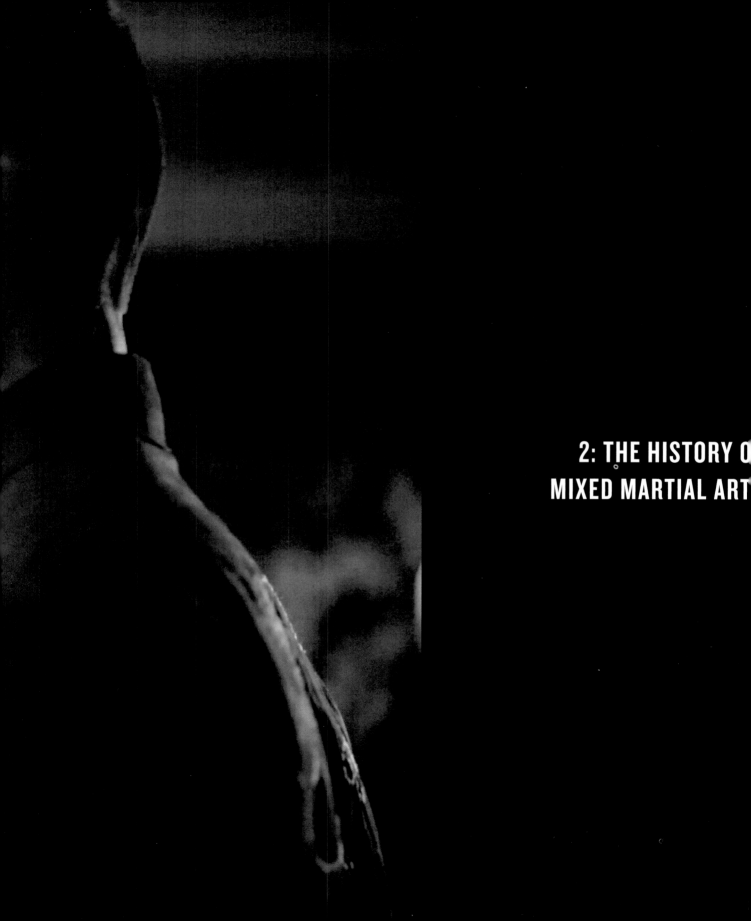

2: THE HISTORY OF MIXED MARTIAL ART

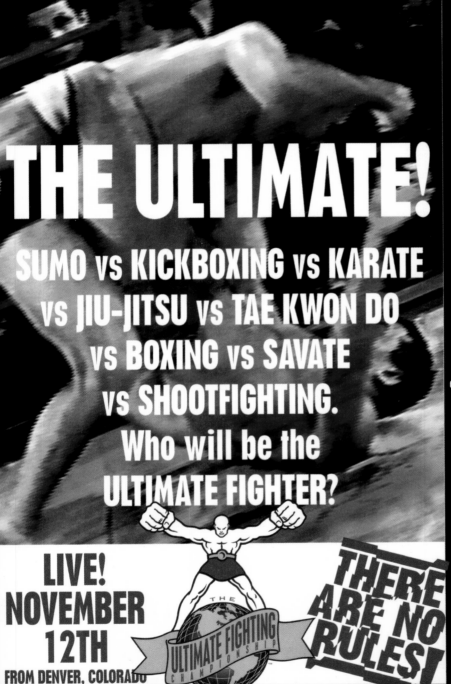

ROYCE GRACIE
0 LBS. 6'1"
DeJANEIRO, BRAZIL
& WORLD JIU-JITSU
HT-HEAVYWEIGHT
PION-RIO DeJANEIRO
JITSU FEDERATION
13-0

PATRICK SMITH
7 LBS. 6'2"
DENVER, CO
TAI KWON DO
WEIGHT CHAMPION
SABAKI CHALLENGE
17-2

EILA TULI
0 LBS. 6'2"
ONOLULU, HI
UMO WRESTLER,
P 100 MAKUSHITA
LASS JAPANESE
PRO SUMO
ASSOCIATION

ZANE FRAZIER
32 LBS. 6'6"
OLLYWOOD, CA
PER HEAVYWEIGHT
CHAMPION
ORLD KICKBOXING
FEDERATION
10-0, 9 KO's
KENPO KARATE

GERARD GORDEAU
216 LBS. 6'5"
AMSTERDAM, NETHERLANDS
WORLD HEAVY WEIGHT
SAVATE CHAMPION
L'ASSOCIATION SAVATE
DE LA MONDE
27-4

ART JIMMERSON
196 LBS. 6'1"
ST. LOUIS, MO
BOXER,
N. AMERICAN IBF
CRUISERWEIGHT
CHAMPION
29-5, 20 KO's

KEVIN ROSIER
265 LBS. 6'4"
CHEEKTOWAGA, NY
KICKBOXER,
3X WORLD KICKBOXING
ASSOCIATION-WORLD
SUPER HEAVYWEIGHT
CHAMPION

KEN SHAMROCK
220 LBS. 6'0"
LOCKEFORD, CA
#1 RANKED
SHOOTFIGHTER
IN THE WORLD,
JAPANESE
PANCRASE
ASSOCIATION

THE ULTIMATE!
SUMO vs KICKBOXING vs KARATE vs JIU-JITSU vs TAE KWON DO vs BOXING vs SAVATE vs SHOOTFIGHTING.
Who will be the ULTIMATE FIGHTER?

LIVE! NOVEMBER 12TH
FROM DENVER, COLORADO

THE ULTIMATE FIGHTING CHAMPIONSHIP

THERE ARE NO RULES!

EXCLUSIVELY ON PAY-PER-VIEW!

"The ending is nearer than you think, and it is already written. All that we have left to choose is the correct moment to begin."
—ALAN MOORE, *V FOR VENDETTA*

THE EARLIEST ACCOUNTS of competitive combat reside in stone carvings, oral histories, and literature. Egyptian hieroglyphs depict soldiers boxing, while Greek mythology tells us the god Apollo invented sport-grappling when he fought Forvanta, a prince chosen to represent humanity. Of course Apollo easily pummeled Forvanta to death, but, hey, the man's legend persists. Even Homer jumped on the bandwagon with *The Iliad*, when at Patroclus's funeral games, Epeus and Euryalus fought for a prized mule. But it's the 23rd Olympic Games in 688 B.C. that provide verifiable records of a primitive form of boxing, and the 648 B.C. Games that boast the sport of pankration, a combination of boxing and wrestling similar to today's mixed martial arts.

These early celebrations of competitive combat mirror our current fascination with MMA. Just as we lionize our champions, the ancient Greeks also revered their fighters. Take Theogenes, the first athlete to earn Olympic gold in both boxing and pankration. Over two decades the legendary pugilist defeated more than fourteen hundred opponents. Of course he probably fought his share of squibs—weaklings thrown into the arena to entertain royal partygoers—but still, given the streak, given the Olympic laurels, it's hard not to crown Theogenes the godfather of MMA. Throughout his life fans erected statues to honor him, and following his death they worshipped him as a healing deity.

Post-Theogenes, let's drop in on Alexander the Great just as he invades India, circa 326 B.C., bringing with him not only swords and archery but also Greek culture: art, cuisine, mythology, sporting events—including pankration. Buddhist monks, chilling in their temples, watched the army practice pankration in the village square. They watched and

learned, keen on the unarmed combat because their honor system prohibited the use of weapons. Records from the era are scant, so from here it's a matter of conjecture. A predominant theory holds that over decades these monks drilled the techniques and, applying their knowledge of anatomy and momentum, evolved the "sport" into something more subtle, more deadly, thus birthing the art of jiu-jitsu.

The sun scorches, the sky is vast, and monks wander. From India our monks roamed the Asian spice routes, arrived in China, and taught their brethren the art. Chinese practitioners ferried the techniques across the East China Sea, and once in Japan, jiu-jitsu embedded itself into the country's martial arts culture.

At least that's what we think. What we *know* is that in 1532 Hisamori Takenouchi, a samurai from the famed Takeda clan, opened the first Japanese jiu-jitsu school, and four centuries later Otavio Mitsuyo Maeda, a Japanese businessman, moved to Brazil and there taught Carlos Gracie the art of jiu-jitsu. Carlos taught his brothers, and Gracie jiu-jitsu (also called Brazilian jiu-jitsu, or BJJ)—the forebear of modern MMA—was born.

THE BIRTH OF UFC

In the late 1980s a VHS tape circulated through the martial arts underground. Copied and recopied, passed hand to hand in locker rooms and dojos, the tape would land in your lap and you'd rush home and jam it into the deck. After the static, a warning appeared—*"To avoid injury, do not attempt these techniques without the supervision of a qualified instructor . . ."*—followed by the title screen: *"Gracie Jiu-Jitsu in Action."* If you're impatient, like me, you'd fast-forward through the scrolling history of jiu-jitsu, past black-and-white footage of old-time judo, to a segment titled "Jiu-Jitsu vs. Karate."

The lo-fi video footage shows a slim Rorion Gracie, a Brazilian jiu-jitsu practitioner and instructor, in a traditional *gi,* squaring off against a karate fighter. Rorion

UFC 1 poster.

circles, feints, then tackles him to the ground. From here it's a pathetic scene. The karate fighter tries to punch, kick, cover his face to avoid shots. But it's no use. Rorion mounts his back, slips a forearm under his neck, chokes him, and it's lights out. The remaining fights follow a similar script. A judo practitioner, a boxer, a wrestler, a brawl on the beach—in each instance a Gracie family member dodges blows, clinches his opponent and wrestles him down, slaps him like a child, then chokes him or nearly breaks an arm before the guy taps in submission.

As the tape ended, you sat in silence, but the message was harsh and loud: the Gracie family challenged any combatants, anywhere, anytime. *You want some of this?!*

Art Davie watched the tape and answered the call—not as a fighter but as a promoter. Years of advertising work taught Davie to recognize opportunity, and stoked on the possibilities he arranged a meeting with Rorion Gracie, wherein he pitched *War of the Worlds*, a combat tournament featuring fighters from every discipline. Rorion signed on, and Davie drafted notable Hollywood director John Milius (also a Gracie jiu-jitsu student) to serve as creative director. The team designed and trademarked the eight-sided cage (known as the Octagon), then changed the name of the tournament to *Ultimate Fighting Championship*.

Next, they met with production companies. HBO and Showtime declined, but SEG, a small pay-per-view production unit, liked the concept. Fast-forward a few months. On November 12, 1993, the *Ultimate Fighting Championship* debuted in Denver, Colorado, and eighty-six thousand home viewers paid to watch. The response exceeded all expectations. "That show was only supposed to be a one-off," Dana White said, "but it did so well on pay-per-view they decided to do another, and another. Never in a million years did these guys think they were creating a sport."

But with that seminal broadcast, a sport was born. Or so it now seems. Truth is, comb the records and you'll find scattered accounts of MMA bouts dating back to the early 1900s, when Brazilian circus promoters hawked *Vale Tudo* (Portuguese translation: "anything goes") battles under the big tent. And this begs the question—when does an underground pursuit qualify as a sport?

Throughout the world, kids play soccer with duct-tape balls on empty fields. Forget the clubs and the stadiums; it's a sport, right? Well, yes and no. In terms of rules and scores and victory celebrations, yes. But as a social institution studied and dissected by sociologists, no.

This is important because recounting the history of MMA, there's always a critic pointing to some earlier event or some unsung fighter: *Whoa, whoa, what about those early Merikan contests in Japan?* and *WTF, you just dissing Sergio Batarelli?*

Exceptions don't make the rule. As stated earlier, this isn't an MMA encyclopedia but more of an exploration of the rising sport as social institution, e.g., gyms opening in every town, kids training and competing in leagues, evolving techniques and philosophies, teams and sponsors, government sanctioning, a defined path to stardom, the inclusion of women, and everyday folk just one, maybe two, degrees of separation from the subculture.

So there it is. *UFC 1* detonates, and during those first few years, ask anyone on the street about MMA, and *if* he knows anything, after a moment he probably nods and says, "Oh yeah, isn't that the skinny dude in a white *gi* that choked everyone out?"

Phase I: That Skinny Dude in a *Gi* (Royce Gracie)

In the parking lot, Royce Gracie opens his trunk. I peer over his shoulder while he picks through rifles and pistols, fills a shoulder bag, dumps in ammo, and turns to me, grinning like a kid at Christmas. I'd heard from his friend Evaldo Lima that Royce was an avid marksman, so while in Toronto for *UFC 152* in September 2012, cageside I told him that after midnight our crew was flying to Maine so we could test Dana's cache on the firing range. He raised his hand, stopping me, and motioned for Dana to hear this. Squinting across the Octagon, Royce pointed out tiny markers in the audience—not heads *per se* but a cup of soda, a raised camera. "Forget jiu-jitsu, guys, from this far I could pick off that, and that. I love to shoot. You guys want, I'll show you, we should go shooting."

So here I am, following him into the Sharpshooter target facility in Torrance, California. Royce struts ahead with the most carefree gait, but it's got little to do with guns or targets—the guy is always stoked. Which makes it hard to fathom why, for the first UFC tournament, Rorion selected *this* Gracie to represent the family. After all, Helio had fathered seven sons, all jiu-jitsu black belts, and no question oldest brother Rickson was the obvious choice: muscular and fierce, a decade prior to *UFC 1* Rickson had choked out the infamous Rei Zulu, a 230-pound beast, before twenty thousand fans. Royce was the complete opposite: a slender 175 pounds at six-foot-one, and compared with the heavyweight savages he would face in the cage, he hardly appeared up to the challenge.

But that was the point. "I picked Royce because he was so young and skinny," Rorion told me. "If Rickson won the tournament everyone would say, 'Oh, it's not jiu-jitsu that won, it's this monster.' But Royce, he was just a kid. Anyone would fight him on the street."

Helio's lifelong goal, and the goal embraced by his children, was to prove Gracie jiu-jitsu as the supreme combat system. Prove and spread his beloved art around the world. Understand, Helio grew up a fragile and sickly boy, plagued by panic attacks, and as an adult he weighed only 138 pounds. But mastering jiu-jitsu increased his confidence, relieved his ailments, and earned him fame in Brazil and Japan. If jiu-jitsu improved his life to such a degree, he couldn't miser-like hoard that knowledge. Think of the positive impact of spreading the discipline throughout a given city, country, continent. Or the world.

So skinny Royce, wearing his traditional *gi*, entered the cage, and throughout the night his Gracie jiu-jitsu easily bested boxing, shootfighting, and karate. Those three wins earned Royce $50,000. But more important, they forever etched his name in the history books as the first UFC champion. He went on to dominate *UFC 2* and *4*, and he is the only fighter to win three UFC tournaments.

Now, at the target station, Royce's son Khonry, still in high school, unfurls a zombie poster. He clips it to a string and zips it off into the range. Royce waves me into the booth. No, I don't wanna shoot first. *What if I suck? I'm gonna look like a fool, and I'll never hear the end of this.* He hands me a Glock, and I raise the gun and squint down the barrel. Royce watching. Khonry watching. Which is just great—it feels like auditioning for a spot on the team. So trying to steady the gun (it's shaking) and keep my arms loose (they're tensed), I single out a one-eyed wraith and squeeze.

Bap! Bap! Bap! Bap! Bap!

Lowering the safety goggles, I spot a small rip in the poster's corner. *That's it?!* Twenty-five yards out, even given *Night of the Living Dead* peril, we're goners. Royce steps beside me, but the smile is gone. Now he's the patient instructor: Here, spread your feet, bend your knees, lean in to the pistol.

Listen, I swear, I've shot guns plenty, I'm not this bad. It's the pressure. So I squeeze off a few more. Blow through a zombie's shoulder, but like that's worth a damn during an apocalypse.

I suck.

Royce takes the pistol, pats my back. At the booth he squares his legs and shoulders, exhales like a Zen master, and squeezes off seven shots. Each bullet tears through a zombie wielding an axe. Saved by a black belt in jiu-jitsu *and* marksmanship.

Khonry steps up with a desert-camo assault rifle, aims through the scope, and decimates another walker. He zips the poster back into the booth and declares himself the winner. *Ah, Dad, look at all these hits, I so beat you!* Royce sighs, tell him to keep dreaming, and points out his son's errant shots.

After a bit, they both look to me, as if I'm qualified to judge.

I just shrug.

—

The morning after *UFC 1* Royce woke to a new life. No screaming mobs or *Tonight Show* offers, but the requests poured in for self-defense seminars—not just from martial arts schools, but also sheriff's departments and military bases. And these law enforcement types were more than happy to take Royce shooting. Hence his skills on the firing range.

Twenty years later, most weekends find Royce jetting around the globe, dispensing his knowledge to eager students: New York, Florida, Paris, Kuwait. Who wouldn't want to learn from the master?

In the years following the inaugural UFC tournament, jiu-jitsu evolved and fractured along various fault lines: the original Gracie jiu-jitsu, MMA jiu-jitsu, and sport jiu-jitsu. Gracie jiu-jitsu schools emphasize self-defense training in the traditional *gi*. MMA jiu-jitsu schools, such as 10th Planet, ditch the *gi* and emphasize a more cage-based approach. Sport schools prepare students for the countless regional, national, and international *gi* tournaments, focusing on overly technical moves that are often not practical against an opponent dropping elbows or knees.

"What use is points in a street fight?" Royce complained when I asked about jiu-jitsu competitions. "Most of those guys don't know how to get out of a basic headlock. Sure, they know X-guard, or the *berimbolo*, but how's that gonna help when a guy's punching you in the face?"

But more than teaching adults to best thugs in a dark alley, Royce enjoys working with children. "My father showed how jiu-jitsu transforms a person. Learning, practicing, and working hard teaches discipline and confidence. These kids grow to respect others and make positive contributions. That's the only way to change the world—one child at a time."

Top: With Royce Gracie at the Sharpshooter target facility in Torrance, California.
Bottom: Royce and his son Khonry admire their handiwork.

Helio passed away in 2009. I ask Royce, in light of MMA's worldwide takeover, how his father viewed his legacy. Royce pauses, clearly remembering his mentor: "He didn't like the new rules, the weight classes, and the judging; after all, MMA was meant to reproduce a street fight. But he was proud, and he respected the sport."

—

After Royce won his third tournament, in 1994, MMA found itself mired in controversy. In 1997, Senator John McCain viewed a tape of *UFC 1*, publicly called it "human cockfighting," then campaigned to ban subsequent events. Other politicians joined the parade, and most states refused to sanction the tournaments. After two years of high-profile scrutiny and declining revenues, Art Davie and his partners sold the company to SEG. Throughout the 1990s the new owners welcomed the bad publicity, believing the attention lent underground credibility. But this stance only isolated the sport. Cable providers refused to carry the broadcasts, and the promoters were forced to hold the events in less-lucrative jurisdictions, such as New Orleans and Colorado. Even the fighters devolved—from single-sport tacticians garbed in traditional attire, they now by and large resembled professional wrestlers: burly, mustached, rage-faced lumberjacks. None more so than Tank Abbott.

Phase II: The Pit Fighters (Tank Abbott)

"By far the greatest number of spontaneous synchronistic phenomena that I have had occasion to observe and analyze can easily be shown to have a direct connection with an archetype. This, in itself, is an irrepresentable, psychoid factor of the collective unconscious."

—CARL J. JUNG

Royce Gracie mentors the next generation.

It's a cool summer night and I'm hurrying down Main Street in Huntington Beach, California, an hour late for beers with a friend. I step into the Aloha Grill and scan the crowd for my boy. I don't see him, and just as I'm ducking out I hear raucous laughter from the corner. Standing in the center of an entourage is a brawny, goateed guy in a Hawaiian shirt, raising his glass and—

It's David "Tank" Abbott, the former UFC fighter. Which shouldn't surprise me. Brazil might've birthed Gracie jiu-jitsu, but Huntington Beach in the mid-1990s begat a slew of early MMA standouts: Kimo Leopoldo, "Razor" Rob McCullough, Tito Ortiz, Jason Miller, Quinton "Rampage" Jackson, Tiki Ghosn, and Ricco Rodriguez.

Tank first stepped into the cage at *UFC 6*, held in Casper, Wyoming, in July 1995. A bear of a fighter, in that first bout he swarmed John Matua, a 400-pound Kapu Kuialua specialist, unloading blow after blow, and finishing the giant in eighteen seconds. Next round he stormed Paul Varelans with an overhand right, tackled him into the cage, wrestled him to the mat, and in typical MMA style mounted and pounded him—but then, never seen this before or since (rewind that footage)—Tank casually sat up and dropped his knee on Varelans's face, and with his fingers he gripped the cage and compressed his knee like a compactor. For a moment he looked into the audience, flashed a *"Hey, want to see something neat?"* grin, and lifted on the fence, sinking his knee until Varelans's eyes bulged. The announcer groaned, "He's kneeing Varelans in the head, and he's enjoying doing it . . ." To which his sidekick responded, "He's smiling at the crowd!" Tank wasn't just smiling, he was laughing . . . LAUGHING at the crowd! *Yeowww, how fun is this!* But then, like a bully growing bored on the playground, he released the fence and close-fist bombed Varelans's temple. Once, twice, three times, and the referee leapt in and stopped the action. TKO.

In the post-fight interviews Tank was jolly, challenging all comers with disdain and scarcely masked rage. The fans loved it. Loved the beer-belly physique and the motorcycle-gang goatee. Loved the bluster and the maniacal aggression. Dan Severn best summarized our boy: "I watched Tank Abbott knock out a sumo [fighter] with one punch, and as the sumo laid there his body stiffened, and Tank struck him again, and I kept thinking there's a man that doesn't have much of a conscience."

Researching this book I'd come across videos of Tank slugging the heavy bag, bench-pressing six hundred pounds. I'd heard he hangs out in Huntington Beach bars, but a friend warned, "Watch your ass. Tank gets drunk, he gets mean. You won't be the first dude he's thrown through a window." But I don't care—I need to talk to him.

The bar is packed, with just a single empty stool one removed from Tank. So I wander up and sit beside an old man, and as the meek interloper I order a shot. Don't look over, just blend in. The glass hits the bar, I down it and take a long breath. My nerves must translate as exhaustion, like that drink is the only good thing in the world, because the old man turns his white goatee my way and eyes my wedding ring. "Yeah, son," he quips, "marriage is hard, I know. Forty-six years, I know. Here, let's have us another."

And that's how it went—me drinking with this old-timer, waiting for an opening with Tank.

Did I mention the bartender's golden pitching arm? How he poured our glasses to the rim, Stoli and Jack, Stoli and Jack, round after round? As we drank, the lights pulsed, or maybe that was the music; it's all a blur . . . The old man slapped my shoulder, told me to cheer up, and, shouting over Bob Seger, here's a bit of what he said:

"—So you're from New Orleans. Great city, had some good times in the French Quarter."

"—No, it's Don, name is Don. Want another?"

"—Katrina, that must'a been a bitch. Can't even imagine what that's like."

"—Well, I coached football at the local junior college close to thirty years. Coached defensive line and linebackers. Loved it. You play?"

"—Take what you can, son. That's the way of the world. If you don't take it, no one gonna hand it to you."

"—Yeah, I hear you, kids can be stubborn. Raised three of 'em, so I know. Just gotta let 'em find their own way."

"—Your daughter's how old? . . . Oh, you started young. Damn."

"—Yeah, I hear you, daughters can break your heart, but sons, they'll give you heartburn. And I know. On weekends I kept $10,000 in the dresser, for bail. Serious. I couldn't really afford the money, being a teacher, but what can you do?"

"—Family's more important than anything. Don't lose sight of that, son. Shit. I miss my wife. Forty-six years we were married. Love of my life. She passed, and I was mad, mad as hell she left me."

"—Come on, drink up. Thought you were from New Orleans!"

"—No question, family comes first. Hell, that's the reason I'm visiting from Colorado, came to see this one—"

With that Don leaned back, hitched his thumb toward Tank. Tank glared at me with narrowed eyes, and that none-too-pleased smirk.

Oh shit.

Clearly, I was in no shape to properly interview the father, much less request an audience with the son. We were at maximum risk of an inappropriate comment or perceived slight, and drunk or sober I'm always good for a few of those. I started to apologize: "Hey, I left my number a few times. I understand you don't like reporters, and that's okay, that's understandable, but I'm a fan . . ."

And to my shock, Tank most graciously nods, tells me this is his hangout, he never misses happy hour.

Fast-forward to the next night: a packed bar again, Tank holding court in his corner. Only now the seat beside him is empty. We shake hands, I sit, and the entourage disperses.

"So what's it mean to be a fighter?" I ask.

Tank sips his drink, smiles. "Don't over-intellectualize it. It doesn't fucking matter. Some things work, some things don't. Don't intellectualize what you think martial arts is. Whatever works, works. It matters what kind of person you are."

What does that mean? He just shakes his head, exasperated. He says something about *the warrior*, and the warrior's code: honor, courage. Just what you'd expect from a fighter. *Okay, Grasshopper, you must demonstrate honor, courage . . .*

But then he pauses, and mulls the line he just fed me. "When I said I was a warrior, I did not realize I was opening myself up to include these people that I don't think are warriors . . . because they are not."

All right, here we go, the real Tank peeking from behind the curtain. "In what respect?" I say.

He rolls his massive shoulders. "Tito would call himself a warrior. But Tito Ortiz is the biggest pussy, dirt bag. . ." Tank reels off a grocery list of pejoratives before adding "For him to say he's a warrior—don't put me in that class. If Tito walked through that door right now, and he saw me, he'd turn that tail and duck out. That's not a warrior. I never turned down a fight."

—

UFC 11.5, or the *Ultimate Ultimate 2* tournament, was held in Birmingham, Alabama, in December 1996. In his quarterfinal bout, the bell sounded and Tank charged Steve "The Sandman" Nelmark, landed a right, and from the center of the ring Nelmark stumbled back into the cage. Tank attacked, swinging. They wrestled against the fence. Nelmark wrapped Tank's head in a guillotine, but before he could cinch down Tank lifted the big man overhead and slammed him to the mat. *Boom!* They grappled for a few seconds, then gained their feet. Tank swarmed in typical fashion, blow after blow, backing Nelmark into the cage. In trouble, anything to stop the fury, Nelmark clinched. *Who is this lunatic?!* Having none of that, Tank yanked his arm free,

stepped back, and hooked a fist to Nelmark's temple. In a frightening blur his knees buckled, his body crumpled, neck and elbows twisted in a painful pretzel. And there he lay. His first loss, his last fight. One of the most terrifying knockouts in MMA history.

—

"A man is shaped by his environment," I quip.

Tank lowers his drink and recalls his high school days, when he trawled these very bars, when Huntington Beach was a very different town. I know this is true—old photos testify to graffiti on crumbling walls, skinheads, alleys, the dingy tattoo parlor, motorcycles outside biker bars. But I wonder, *If a warrior is shaped by his environment, what happens when that environment softens?*

Before I can ask, he says, "But these guys don't like to fight. I used to drive around, drinking my beer. I had a van with a thousand-watt stereo, and I would pull up [to a dojo], get out, and go, 'Who wants to fight?' I'm not joking. The *instructor*, the *warrior*, would say, 'Sir, we can't really do that . . .' I'm like, 'You're a fighter, let's fight!' 'Well, our insurance, we can't, we can't' . . . *pffft!* That's why I hate all those guys, they don't fight . . . I don't fight for money. I fight because it's who I am."

Surely he's not calling out the top ranks, is he? Oh, but he is.

"How many of these fighters really fight?" he says. "[Tell] B.J. Penn, 'I'll see you tomorrow at two o'clock in my backyard and we're gonna fight' . . . he wouldn't do it. I have beaten up well over two hundred people in this town."

"So what are you doing now?" I ask.

"Writing. I just completed a thousand-page novel."

WTF?

He smirks. "I've got a degree."

"Your dad, that's right, he was a college professor. "

"Yeah, it started out as an autobiography, but . . ."

For three years Tank says he has holed up in the same

bars he used to terrorize: *then,* bottles smashing and fists flying; *now,* huddled in the corner with headphones, scrawling his story upon legal pad after legal pad. But he found that the narrative kept straying from reality's narrow path into the woods of fiction, and out leapt Walter Fox, the archetypal badass hero.

—

To be fair, history's best fighters, the fighters we will actually stand in line for hours to watch—win/lose/draw—are also history's most brilliant promoters. Ali. Tyson. Sugar Ray Leonard. There's usually only one from each era. And Tank, well, he promoted. Which makes perfect sense, as the man is a *student* of history—along with a stellar fight record he earned a bachelor's degree in history. So he was likely well aware of the fighter lineage. Yes, for the most part he has departed the cage, but he's still ringside, here in this bar, reaching for the mic.

"Walter Fox gets down," he slurs, and there's a twinkle in his eye. God, he's so enjoying this. And that's what I love about him. The man has earned this twilight in this bar, and he's basking in it.

"Any advice for young fighters?"

"If you have a strong wrestling background, you control the fight, then you can strike and punch. And that's when the fun starts."

During *UFC* 8, in Puerto Rico in February 1996, Tank was milling through the crowd. Allan Góes, a jiu-jitsu specialist, made a snarky comment. Starting a beef, Tank lunged, fists flew. Cameras caught the scuffle. UFC promoters suspended him *with pay.* When interviewed about the fracas, Tank responded, "Somebody got smart with me, and, uh, I had to lay the law down, I can't let people talk to me like that . . . if I would have took it further, I'm coming after your ass, and I'll knock on your front door and take care of you. Let's put it this way, you've seen Discovery Channel, you've seen some animals rip apart a gazelle; that's what's gonna happen."

"What do you think of MMA today?"

"I don't watch it," he says.

"???"

"I'm serious. In the old days, it was about who was the baddest fighter . . . now, all these weight classes, these rules. *Pffft.* Nah, I don't know any of the guys."

I rattle off names of fighters, elicit a few remarks.

Brock Lesnar: "Brock Lesnar couldn't beat himself out of a wet paper bag."

Chuck Liddell: "He's about average, he didn't have much power."

Dan Henderson: "[Hendo] needs a stepladder to trim my toenails. You think he could bench six hundred pounds? Of course not. You think he could put up 325 pounds? No."

Chael Sonnen: "I know that guy. One time I was training with Mark Shultz [Olympic and World Champion wrestler], and he was there. He said he could take me down. I rolled my eyes and he shoots a low single on me; sure enough, took me down. Hah!"

Anderson Silva: "No idea who he is."

—

Lying in bed that night, I stare into the darkness, still hearing the din of barroom music and shouting. But that's not why I'm awake. Tonight I met one of the sport's revered pit fighters, and instead of talking technique or the game, he seemed more concerned with engineering his own legend.

Egomaniac or genius?

Yin or yang?

Or perhaps both.

Several times he pointed a finger at me and said, "I live to fight, I don't fight to live." And the way he sneered delivering the line, I could just see him in the bathroom mirror, perfecting his anti-hero delivery.

Carl Jung preached that all folklore, myths, and, yes, *religion* are based on archetypes. The Hero. Trickster. Maiden. Wise Mentor. Anti-Hero. These archetypes are embedded

in our DNA. We empathize, sometimes hate, even worship them. This is Psych 101. And as a college graduate, and especially as an aspiring writer, Tank *must* know this.

Which brought to mind his reply to my final question. "Why has MMA finally taken off worldwide?"

Tank smirked, didn't even have to think. "Because in a bar, or even driving in his car, a dude gets static . . . well, he wants to go off and fuck someone up. But he can't or won't. That's why MMA is so popular—guys can live vicariously through us, the fighters."

Mythology. Religion. Maybe that's why.

Phase III: The Modern Era (Vitor Belfort versus Randy Couture)

No broadcast platform meant no money for purses, for production, or for advertising to the masses. And for fans who watched, the UFC tournaments lost the intriguing diversity. John Milius, in crafting those embryonic events, understood that sporting events provide a social function far and away more important than a shimmering belt. The drama unfolds while *we*, the fans, project our fears, frustrations, and aspirations onto the field of play.

In so many ways the Emperor Vespasian understood this when he commissioned the construction of the Colosseum in ancient Rome, just as his successors understood that every great drama requires a motley cast, and thus they injected slaves from every conquered country into the games. Imagine a production with the same character in every role—boring. The fans need *archetypes* at which to cheer, hiss, and curse. That's why in crafting the inaugural

Me with Don Abbott and Tank Abbott, in Huntington Beach, California.

UFC tournament, Milius and Rorion Gracie selected not only fighters boasting different combat styles but also fighters of various nationalities, wearing diverse garb: an African American in boxing trunks, a Brazilian in a *gi*, a Samoan in a sarong.

Yet, come *UFC 11*, in September 1996, six of the eight fighters were American brawlers culled from the same mold. Aside from the violence, the events offered scant spectacle. If you question this, cue up *UFC 11* and watch two of the top fighters, Tank Abbott and Scott Ferrozzo, plod around the ring. Both fighters were so fat and gassed, their semifinal match is hard to qualify in terms such as *athletic* or *technical*. More barroom brawlers with zero martial arts training. In the end, Ferrozzo's decision victory is irrelevant, as it renders him so exhausted he can't leave the locker room for his final fight with Mark Coleman, and thus via forfeit he hands Coleman the tournament crown.

That changed in February 1997 with *UFC 12*, which heralded the arrival of heavyweight Vitor Belfort, the great Brazilian hope. A nineteen-year-old jiu-jitsu champion under Carlson Gracie, Vitor entered the cage thickly muscled and, well, like something spawned in a lab. Imagine a fight scientist dissecting and improving on Royce Gracie—removing the *gi*, adding thirty pounds of dense muscle, gifting him with lightning punches, then draping over his shoulders a Brazilian flag. The young hero. A perfect archetype to recapture the glory for the motherland.

And recapture he did. Vitor blitzed through two American opponents, downing Tra Telligman in just 1:17 and Scott Ferrozzo in 0:43. Fans christened him "The Phenom." But the kid was more than just a freakish aberration—here stood *the* prototype for our modern MMA fighter: highly conditioned, athletically gifted, with mad jiu-jitsu skills and world-class striking.

For *UFC 13* in May 1997, promoters hyped a super-fight pitting Tank versus Vitor: the old guard versus the new. From the referee's signal Tank claimed center-ring and attempted to manhandle Vitor; but the kid was too strong,

too fast, and in seconds Tank lay belly down on the mat, trying to block the blows pelting his head and neck. TKO fifty-two seconds into the first round.

So here's Vitor, a quantum evolutionary leap. Punctuated equilibrium, they call it. Until *UFC 15* in October 1997, when promoters pitted the Brazilian Phenom against Randy Couture, his freakish American twin. While Vitor sweated in a jiu-jitsu dojo, Couture sacrificed and scored on the wrestling mats: state champ in high school, three-time NCAA Division I All-American at Oklahoma State University, sergeant in the U.S. Army, three-time Greco-Roman USA Olympic alternate. Fans dubbed him "Captain America."

Vitor knew of Couture's reputation, and he grew so nervous prior to the bout he refused to leave his trailer. The crowd jeered. Promoters panicked, pleading with his coaches. *Please, he has to fight, Jesus Christ, we flew him here, sold tickets, they'll riot* . . . Randy paced the Octagon, growing more and more confident. All those years of battle, he knew: *I got this guy, he's mine, battles are won and lost in the mind* . . . fifteen minutes ticked off the clock and finally Vitor entered the arena, but it was already over—

After an exciting eight minutes and sixteen seconds, Randy defeated Vitor via TKO, but more important than fight stats or titles, this bout ushered in the modern era of MMA—where *true* mixed martial artists ruled the cage.

THE ZUFFA ACQUISITION

By the late 1990s SEG teetered on a financial cliff. Mounting debts and declining revenues threatened bankruptcy. Dana White, while negotiating a contract for his client, MMA fighter Tito Ortiz, learned that the organization was on the blocks. How Dana mentioned the opportunity to Lorenzo

The Brazilian Phenom vs. Randy Couture, *UFC 15*.

★ HEAVYWEIGHT SUPERFIGHT ★

COUTURE

THE NATURAL

VS.

THE PHENOM

BELFORT

UFC XV   OCTOBER 17, 1997   BAY ST. LOUIS, MISSISSIPPI

★ COLLISION COURSE ★

Fertitta, and Lorenzo's attorneys and accountants urged him to reject the deal—*the UFC holds no assets . . . no promise of solvency . . . fans worldwide have watched and rejected MMA . . . the sport at best will linger on the fringes*—how, despite these advisors, within a month Lorenzo and his brother, Frank, purchased the league in January 2001 for a paltry $2 million, and installed Dana as president—is well-documented history.

But few know the acrimony this purchase caused within the close-knit Fertitta family. Growing up in Las Vegas, I've known Lorenzo most of my life, through intramural sports and local gyms, and I knew his family was close. His father, Frank, was a respected entrepreneur, having bucked conventional wisdom and successfully marketed his off-strip casino to locals. It was a crazy, ingenious business strategy, to offer cheap beers and cheaper meals, cash-your-check promotions, slot tournaments.

The casino flourished, but despite Mr. Fertitta's hectic schedule he attended every football practice and game, and every week he hosted the entire football team for dinner. And no matter what, his children ate Sunday meals together, a tradition that gathers the extended family to this day.

So when Lorenzo and Frank spurned their father's counsel and employed his own against-the-grain business strategy to MMA, it was a big deal.

Zuffa is Italian for "scuffle." This is the name the Fertitta brothers chose for the entity that would control the UFC. While this can be read as an apt descriptor for their new endeavor, it also signals their approach to business: a willingness to roll up sleeves and knock heads—relentless aggression coupled with extreme discipline.

Unlike the prior UFC owners, the Fertittas brought years of hardened business experience into the cage. Since the late 1980s, brother Frank served as president of Station Casinos, growing a solitary local casino into one of the largest public gaming entities in the world. In 1993, Lorenzo earned an MBA from New York University and afterward joined the company as an executive. Come the

millennium, they knew how to grow a business.

But just what had they bought? Let's see: a bankrupt organization hemmed in by recalcitrant politicians, events outlawed in nearly every jurisdiction and blacklisted by cable providers. But despite seven years of misrule and decline, post-Vitor the *sport* of MMA had progressed—UFC cards featured more international fighters, and those fighters increasingly entered the cage versed in both striking and grappling.

Here were their immediate goals:

1. Land a pay-per-view broadcast deal.
2. Work *with* government and seek state sanctioning—specifically in Nevada, where hosting events in conjunction with major casinos, as in boxing, might prove lucrative.
3. Improve the live fight experience.
4. Increase advertising.
5. Make Dana the public face of UFC.

None of which would prove easy.

Like father like son: Vitor and Davi Belfort.

3: MARTIAL ARTS STYLES

"Absorb what is useful, discard w[ ]s not, add what is uniquely your own."

—BRUCE LEE

ALMOST EVERYONE in the industrialized world has, at the very least, strolled past a television and glimpsed two fighters trading blows in the cage. This first look is often so overwhelming, so shocking, so thrilling, that the subtle instincts governing those feints, kicks, and takedowns go unseen. I didn't enjoy watching MMA until I gained at least a cursory understanding of the techniques and strategies.

So let's delve deeper, sink beneath muscles and bones, down into the neural pathways, where techniques and hairtrigger responses take root, each lightning riposte honed over thousands of gym hours. Sure, raise a fist to strike me and I'll flinch. That's Darwinian. But learning to block properly or roll with a punch, that's a wholly different process. Take the simple jab: feet shoulder-width apart, weight on toes, knees bent and torso turned, hands raised, chin on chest, push off the rear foot and shift hips while thrusting a semi-relaxed arm along the horizontal plane, then closing in on the target, clench that fist, and quickly retrieve the arm along the same horizontal plane to block a counter.

Think you're gonna memorize and call up that checklist in the heat of battle? Think again. I'm omitting at least twenty other movements critical to a mechanically correct jab—and in the cage, under the hot lights and in front of screaming fans, there's no time to ponder.

That means drill, drill, and, yeah, drill some more. Drill until that jab is more natural than the breath you just took. And we're not talking mere shadowboxing in front of your bathroom mirror, but drilling for years under a skilled trainer's guidance. A trainer who watches and constantly corrects—*step here, no, angle that foot and bend your knee*—because, as Vince Lombardi said, "It's not practice that

---

Bruce Lee, the godfather of MMA.

makes perfect, but perfect practice makes perfect."

So just *what* does a fighter drill?

Recall the inaugural UFC, and Royce mopping up with jiu-jitsu, dispelling all doubts. But over two decades the world moved on, and during the ensuing years fighters universally added jiu-jitsu to their arsenals, leveling the Gracie advantage. No more *gis* in the cage. No more skinny fighters facing three-hundred-pound monsters. We're talking weight classes, timed rounds, leather gloves, standardized rules, and, yes, fighters trained in grappling *and* striking.

But this was a process, at times awkward and stuck in the bog, and at times awesome. As with Royce, occasionally fighters from other combat disciplines, at least for a spell, dominated the cage—that is until other combatants co-opted the new advantage. This viral cycle of infection, adaptation, and incorporation continued for decades until, *voila!,* the genetic hybrid that is modern MMA emerged as its own sport.

Through exultant victories and heartrending defeats, it's now clear that before entering the cage, at least at the elite level, a fighter must train and near-master not only jiujitsu but also muay Thai, wrestling, and a bit of boxing. A weakness in any area renders a fighter vulnerable.

On a final note, any exploration of *style* requires a discourse of not only the techniques required to compete at the elite levels of MMA but also the decade-long path a fighter hews into the cage. Now, understand that I'm talking the rule, not the wayward exception, when I say no chance in hell a twenty-two-year-old warehouse clerk who has never studied a combat discipline is going to one morning join a gym and work his way toward a UFC contract. Anything is possible. But by and large fighters enter the cage after years of training one of the numerous combat disciplines. However that doesn't mean each path is equal.

After scouring official records and speaking to countless trainers and fighters, I was shocked by my conclusions. Again, put away the pitchforks, I'm not addressing the exceptions. Like many, I assumed jiu-jitsu was the superior path, as nearly every UFC fighter holds a black belt in the art. But

BRASIL ★ JAPÃO

ESTADIO DO MARACANA

OUTUBRO

23

1951

HELIO
GRACIE

MASAHIKO
KIMURA

the truth is, jiu-jitsu is just too passive. We all know the tired metaphors—a blacksmith pounding red-hot steel, molten metal burning away the impurities. But practice a discipline and more than acquiring mastery, the endeavor molds a fighter's demeanor. And quite often *demeanor* trumps skills.

MMA is a brutally tough sport. That's evident, but it's not just the fights, it's the endless training sessions, head games, and relentless media scrutiny. So you have to ask, Does a particular discipline, regardless of combat effectiveness, adequately prepare a fighter to seize the belt?

JIU-JITSU

Last we left Otavio Mitsuyo Maeda, he had just taught Carlos Gracie the art of jiu-jitsu, and from there Carlos taught his brothers—all except Helio, the youngest. Poor Helio was so frail and sickly that on doctor's orders he could only watch. But watch he did. Unbeknownst to the others he studied their techniques, working the mechanics in his mind, parsing each movement and isolating a weakness here, a potential variant there, so years later, when Carlos failed to show for a class, Helio stepped in as teacher. The students praised him, and from thereon he taught at the family academy.

But all was not well with Helio. Due to his smallish stature he couldn't pull off the moves executed by stronger opponents, so he modified the techniques, honing the art much like those unarmed Buddhist monks of lore. Intellect over brawn. Leverage over speed. In the end, Helio engineered a system of jiu-jitsu—Gracie jiu-jitsu—so effective that in just a few years he challenged Masahiko Kimura, Japan's greatest jiu-jitsu practitioner, to a fight before twenty thousand rabid Brazilians.

Jujutsu translates from Japanese as "gentle art," but it's more a physical game of chess. Many fans groan when

---

On October 23, 1951, the most important fight in the history of jiu-jitsu was held in Rio de Janeiro.

fighters hit the mat—*wriggling around, grabbing ass,* they say. And I get it. Count me among those bellyachers—that is until I rolled a few times. Then I understood the origami-like *art* unfolding on the mat. After just two sessions the scales fell from my eyes. *Position Before Submission* is a common jiu-jitsu mantra, and what it means is, during all that ass-grabbing, the fighters are actually struggling for superior positions from which to attempt a highlight-worthy armbar, foot lock, or choke. No doubt it's subtle. Passing a knee just inches here, sliding hips there, makes all the difference and often determines the victor.

To demonstrate the four basic positions, here's Rener and Ryron Gracie, the eldest grandsons of Helio and two of the most respected MMA commentators in the biz. Together they host "Gracie Breakdown," a monthly segment on the Fuel TV show *UFC Ultimate Insider.*

Closed or Full Guard. Despite how this appears, Ryron (in white) is actually in a dominant position because his legs control Rener's hips. However, he must also "break" Rener's upright posture by pulling him low—or else suffer punches and elbows to the face.

Breaking the Posture. Ryron breaks Rener's posture. Now he can move toward a submission—armbar, triangle, omaplata.

Side Control. Ryron controls the hips with his own knee and elbow, thereby trapping Rener. From here Ryron can drop elbows and punches or attempt a submission.

Half Guard. Rener "half" passes through Ryron's full guard, and now he's in a dominant position. From here he must slip his leg free and continue to side control.

Full Mount. This is a desperate situation for Rener. With no leverage or options but to cover his face, he's now Ryron's little brother, subject to whatever punishment Ryron deems appropriate. Rener must try to bridge on his neck, escape his legs, and encircle Ryron's hips, thus re-establishing closed guard, or he won't last long.

Taking the Back. It doesn't get much worse. Ryron is seconds from snaking a forearm under Rener's chin and choking him into oblivion.

There it is. Next time an MMA fight hits the mat, watch the fighters moving for these positions.

After shooting the above photos, I sat with Rener and picked his brain re: the rise of jiu-jitsu, the art's influence on MMA, and how to win a street fight against a giant.

This is just my experience, but it seems that more kids are learning jiu-jitsu than other martial arts—is that accurate, and why?

"Just do the math and count back to the first UFC event. In 1993, karate and tae kwon do were big. But now, this idea of the perfect kick—the perfect spinning back kick, the perfect flying whatever—it's not very reliable in a real fight, and people know that. So you have parents saying, 'Hey, my kid needs to learn self-protection, gain some confidence.' Well, that parent, during every UFC fight, hears Joe Rogan yelling, 'Oh, jiu-jitsu this, jiu-jitsu that.' It's a household term that parents hear far more than karate. So when they

think, *My kid needs to learn something,* it's jiu-jitsu, because that's what they've seen in the cage every weekend. Also, a kid learning jiu-jitsu isn't getting punched and kicked, so there's no worry about concussions."

Online and in gyms I see flyers advertising jiu-jitsu competitions—is there a difference between self-defense jiu-jitsu and sport jiu-jitsu?

"They all spring from the same place. In the 1960s jiu-jitsu competitions started in Brazil. Initially, they trained only self-defense jiu-jitsu, blocking punches, kicks, all that. So [in these first tournaments] they'd compete without strikes in a raw, controlled setting to test their street skills. But then came this importance and emphasis on tournaments, and people started saying, 'What can we do within the confines of these rules, these guidelines, to ensure a victory, even if it means not being as successful in real fights?' That shift took place in the late 1960s, early 1970s, and it's gotten to the point where in many schools 100 percent of the training is for this sort of recreational effectiveness, as opposed to preparing a student for combat against a giant. There are schools you could train at for three years and never learn to block a punch. That's the difference.

"So a sport jiu-jitsu match has no concern for distance. You grab *gis,* sleeves, and belts—all these different things that don't exist in a real fight—and push or pull with no concern for how far the other guy's fist is from you face. In street jiu-jitsu, the number one thing is distance management. It doesn't matter if you're standing or on the ground, in a street fight whoever controls the distance comes out on top."

What does that mean, controlling the distance?

"In a fight, whoever manages the distance between the two subjects will win. If you fight Anderson Silva, the reason he's gonna knock you out is because he's gonna control the distance. You try to close it, and he will say, 'No, I'm here now, I'm there.' He's gonna keep you just out of range from grabbing him and perfectly in range so he can strike you. He's the distance owner of every negotiation—that is, until he gets a wrestler who is more effective at distance management than him. But then, ironically, when someone like Chael [Sonnen], who is a very effective wrestler, gets on top of him, what happens? Anderson pulls Chael close so he can't hit him. During any given sliver of time in a fight someone is controlling the distance. When Chael is on top of Anderson, what does he want? Striking distance. Anderson didn't give it to him. So isn't it fascinating that at any given point during a fight—who's winning? Whoever is controlling the distance. That's the primary rule in self-defense jiu-jitsu."

What do you think about the rise of no-gi jiu-jitsu [when the sport is practiced in surfing trunks and a rash guard, as opposed to a *gi*]?

"Totally logical, makes sense. I never saw the two as separate things. For me jiu-jitsu is whatever I'm wearing—I could be in board shorts or snowboarding gear. It's more about how to defend myself from getting punched in the face. Come at me, and the moment you make a mistake I'm gonna choke you out. That's jiu-jitsu. So the rise [of no-*gi* jiu-jitsu] makes sense given the rise of MMA. But with all these people saying no-*gi* jiu-jitsu is more realistic than *gi*, I don't agree with that at all. I think that is wrong in many ways. Your jiu-jitsu and your self-defense abilities should not be limited by your clothing. If that's the case, how good are you? My grandfather nailed that down very early: if we wear a *gi* when we practice, that doesn't mean we need a *gi* to win or survive. However, training purely with a rash guard and board shorts every time—when you get in a street fight wearing a jacket, and someone grabs your collar [and] starts punching you in the face and you don't know how to deal with the restraint, well . . . So here's my final thought on *gi* versus no-*gi*: training no-*gi* refines your control and submission capabilities, and training [in the] *gi* refines your escape and submission counters."

Is that why so many UFC fighters train in a gi?

"Absolutely. They train in a *gi* because it helps their escapes. Once they get proficient wearing a *gi* and then take

it off, you can't hold them down. If I want to get up from the bottom of a fight, I'm getting up guaranteed because I'm so used to being immobilized with the *gi* that when you take it off, it's like free wings to fly. Straight up.

"But on the submission front, you don't want to become too reliant on the *gi*. Because when you go to no-*gi*, you're in trouble. So what's the ultimate training? Wear a *gi* and train against someone who is not wearing one!"

The original Gracie Jiu-Jitsu in Action *featured Gracie fighters throwing side kicks. Yet I've never seen that in a jiu-jitsu gym—why not?*

Gracie jiu-jitsu includes strikes—however, the strikes are used only as a means to get to what we really want—which is to control the distance. So we use strikes not to win the fight but to better our position. For example, I don't want to stand trading punches with an opponent because if I'm weaker, or he gets lucky, I might get knocked out. So I throw a jab, or a side kick, to measure the distance, and to provoke my opponent's anger, get him to charge so I can close and grab him easier. The strikes are flash-bang entry methods—not, *Oh I'm gonna knock this fool out and win this fight with one punch*. That's an illusion because every time I put myself in range to hit, I am now in range to get hit, and if it's a heavier or stronger attacker, which we must always assume it is, I'm in trouble. Never ever trade blows."

If a young kid with zero prior training tells you he wants to get into MMA, how do you respond?

"Get a purple belt in jiu-jitsu, and don't think about fighting until then. Fighting is like jumping from a plane, and jiu-jitsu is your parachute. What I mean is, you can get in a fight and do all the kickboxing—throw all the flashy punches and kicks you want—but when things get tight, you better pull the rope.

"No question, pound-for-pound the best striker in the world is Anderson Silva, agreed? Well, what's his parachute? It's black-belt distance-management on the ground. That's not muay Thai, that's jiu-jitsu, learned from someone who learned from someone in the family.

"So get a purple belt. A blue belt is decent, you have a little knowledge, you can win a street fight, but not against another savvy grappler or a wrestler who imposes his aggression. But a purple belt, that's safe. At that level you've got enough instinctive reflex, and belief in your moves, that when things get tight and you get punched, your body knows what to do. You don't even think about it, the responses take over. But as a blue belt, you get rocked and you might go back to what you did in third grade—get him in a head lock and hold on for dear life. With a purple belt, you don't do that. You go to your core, to what your body reflexively knows."

What's the best path into the cage?

"If you want to compete in MMA, in addition to jiu-jitsu you gotta learn striking skills. More than a jab and a side kick to close distance, you must learn to knock someone out with a right cross on a moment's notice. Because if you're not banging in there, they don't want to see you fight. So you have to acquire every tool that your opponents are using. You can't enter the cage with a smaller skill set. That means incredible muay Thai, wrestling, endurance—the physical conditioning has to be top notch."

Why does wrestling account for the background of so many UFC fighters?

"The circumstances and judging imposed by MMA favor the wrestler because to most viewers if you are on top you're winning. It's a visual thing, but it's not real. The truth is, you could be on the bottom saving energy, burning your opponent's energy, striking effectively, neutralizing strikes, but for most judges this doesn't matter. It goes back to the sport and what they want for entertainment purposes.

"Wrestling is also such an explosive sport, which translates. I wrestled in high school, and it's six minutes of kill or be killed. I'm not dogging wrestling, it's great. I'm glad I did it. Anybody who has the athleticism and the drive should wrestle. But not everyone has the desire or ability to go in there and crack skulls for however long it takes to become proficient. Jiu-jitsu, on the other hand, is the everyman's art.

That's what makes it special. If you're not a tough animal, no way you're going to wrestle. Think about this: by the time a wrestler reaches the highest level in the NCAA, he's been to hell and back. MMA is no big deal, you've already done the hard work. Now just learn some striking and don't get submitted. You can have a blue belt in jiu-jitsu and survive submissions with a good wrestling background."

So, the best path?

"Train jiu-jitsu since you're five, wrestle when you get to high school, and kickbox the entire time. Wrestling brings the explosive fire, teaches you to impose your will, and that's very different from what jiu-jitsu was designed for; because if we train our jiu-jitsu with that wrestling mindset—*kill or be killed, you gotta get that point, fight for that top position*—we'd ruin the essence of what makes the art so special, which is that a smaller, weaker, less athletic person can survive any attack. That's what it's all about."

What would Helio, your grandfather, think of jiu-jitsu's blossoming across the world?

"He knew it was just a matter of time. In Brazil, before he got here, he was already changing lives. Neighbors, senators, the president, the president's son, they all trained with him. It's crazy huge over there, just like it's becoming here. In terms of self-defense, he knew it was the best thing. Good things always find their way to the top."

MUAY THAI

Muay Thai fighters strike with fists, elbows, knees, and feet, and for this reason the discipline is known as "The Science of Eight Limbs." Like jiu-jitsu, the ancient origins of muay Thai lie shrouded in mist: whether developed by Siamese soldiers losing their weapons on the battlefield, or descended from Sanskrit-era Indian boxing, no one knows.

Nai Khanom Tom was a revered muay Thai warrior. Regarded as the godfather of kickboxing, his statue stands guard in the capital city of Ayutthaya, Thailand. A grim

Buddha warning back all comers. Every day worshippers leave flowers, to pay homage. Here's why. In 1776, the Burmese army captured Ayutthaya and imprisoned thousands of its soldiers. After proclaiming victory, the Burmese king heard boasting about the level of Thai kickboxing: it's world class, unbeatable, an immortal art, and so on. Sick and tired of the rumors he organized a tournament to prove his nation's superiority.

Sound familiar?

Of course it does.

Let's cut straight to the action: after a lengthy introduction, the Burmese champ bows before the throne. The crowd cheers, hailing their hero. The king raises a scepter for silence. Nai Khanom Tom, chosen to represent Thailand,

steps from the throng. Shuffling forward, shy in the limelight, instead of bowing he rises on his toes and whirls this way and that, waving his hands overhead like a Pentecostal snake charmer, performing a traditional pre-fight dance that, holy shit, leaves the audience stunned and frightened. *Who is this black magic dervish?*

Exasperated, the king signals for combat. The Burmese champ circles, fists raised. Nai charges forward in a flurry of elbows, knees, and kicks that backs the champ across the courtyard and lays him out, blank-eyed staring at passing clouds. The crowd moans. *What has befallen our lionhearted hero?*

The king signals for another Burmese challenger, then another, and another. Each lies drooling on the cold marble. In the end, the king crowns Nai Khanom Tom the tournament champion, gifting his freedom as well as the treasure of his choice. Instead of gold Nai selects two wives from the

Court McGee unleashes a flying knee on Dongi "The Ox" Yang during *UFC Fight Night 25*.

king's harem, and to this day the country reveres him as the godfather of muay Thai.

It's fair to remark, at least in passing, that muay Thai resembles karate. But watch side-by-side videos and you'll see karate as a more light-footed samba of deft jabs, circular footwork, and surgical kicks. Which jibes: the Tao of karate emphasizes energy flow and patience, whereas the Tao of muay Thai focuses on explosive aggression, and thus yields a nitrous oxide bang-fest. Think Theogenes dominating his opponent, hurling hammer-fists. *Boom! Boom! Boom!* Muay Thai kickboxers meet center of the ring and throw savage kicks shin-on-shin, spinning elbows that cut foreheads, flying knees.

Despite this brutality a great muay Thai leg kick is a thing of beauty. Not in the classical sense but in that release-of-primal-force sense. Most powerful athletic movements equate to cracking a whip: relax muscles as the whip arcs overhead, increasing in velocity until a last-second wrist snap delivers that *crack!* Same with throwing a baseball. Or hitting a racquetball. Or serving in tennis.

The formula is simple: relaxation equals speed, and speed equals power.

BACKSTAGE UFC

Half an hour before the Michael Bisping versus Brian Stann fight during *UFC 152* in September 2012, I'm roaming backstage, camera in-hand, security guards at every corner, checking my credentials. After my first UFC fight, I traveled with Dana to an out-of-town event and over lunch told him I wanted to shoot photos. It was just before the pre-fight press conference, and we were at a pizza joint. He as usual was texting on his antiquated flip phone: fork in one hand, the other thumb flying across tiny keys. That's how slammed things get in the days leading up to an event—endless production questions, media requests, shouts from friends—so the moment there's a break in the responses, he sneaks another bite.

"Cool if I shoot photos?" I ask.

He gives me a no-look nod.

"You sure?"

"Dude, I don't care," he whispers, but he's so lost in his phone I feel compelled to press.

"Of everything, like backstage, the fighters warming up in their change rooms—"

I'm pushing because I recognize the gravity of this moment in history. That's the beauty of wife/kids/job— you learn that all of life's big-or-small moments are fleeting, and hesitation leaves you squinting in the rearview mirror, regretting you didn't chronicle what just transpired. *This too shall pass.*

"—that cool with you?"

"Pass me the water," he says, so start shooting I did.

That first night I was skittish, glancing over my shoulder and wondering how far to push it: ducking into dressing rooms, roaming cageside, poking my lens into the post-fight medical tent. Staff stopped me at every corner, told me no cameras allowed backstage. Photographers are confined to the Octagon.

Well, I'm not much of a listener.

Anatomy of a Kick

I enter the change room just as Michael Bisping unloads several muay Thai kicks on the bags, each shot backing Tiki Ghosn, his trainer, across the mat. *Bam! Bam! Bam!* As a teenager Bisping won the Pro British kickboxing title. After transitioning to MMA he beat ten straight opponents, knocking out or submitting every one. During season 3 of *The Ultimate Fighter* he won the show as a light heavyweight. Now he sits atop the UFC light heavyweight rankings, awaiting a title shot. Bisping heads a wave of elite European fighters, and after a decade of throwing muay Thai kicks, it's as though his body's absorbed all the kick's nuances and now it's merely a matter of summoning his chi—a split-second furrowed brow and intense glare, then a coiling of the hips, a short step, and *Bam!*

Bisping demonstrates a correct muay Thai kick as Tiki watches: he steps before the target, foot angled forty-five degrees in the direction of his momentum, and rising on the ball of his foot, he lifts his leg and quick-shifts his hips, thus snapping the kick *through* the target.

It's a difficult movement, totally unlike kicking a ball across a field. But drill the kick ten thousand times and in a bout, I'm told, the recall is pure autopilot.

Why is this kick so important?

For head shots, the physiology is intuitive. Throw an uppercut to the chin and—as though detaching battery cables—an opponent slumps to the canvas. That's why the chin is coined *the button*. A targeted shot whiplashes the head backward, the gray sponge sloshes against the skull, and the light bulb that signifies consciousness blinks out.

Fairly straightforward, but to truly appreciate the damage inflicted by a proper muay Thai kick requires a more detailed anatomy primer. So cageside between fights I asked Dr. Jeff Davidson, UFC's lead doctor, to explain. He pointed to my lower back. "Longest, thickest nerve in the body," he shouted over the music, "like an electrical wire to the central nervous system, it weaves through this dense muscle [buttocks], twists down along the femur, and emerges surface-level *here* [right above the knee] for just a few inches before retreating deep into the calf."

That's the body's second *button*. The leg button. Slam a shin into this area and it's more than just intense cramping pain, it's a shock that radiates groin to foot. One solid kick and a fighter's limping. Which slows down his double-legs, weakens his punches. Renders him gun-shy. Unable to weight that leg for an effective counter-kick. A few more strikes and he'll drop.

Watch highlights from *World Extreme Cagefighting* (*WEC*) *48* in April 2010, featuring the Urijah Faber versus José Aldo title fight. Early on Aldo steps and winds up that

Michael Bisping, leg kick. (Mural by El Mac and RETNA)

whip, *crack!,* and kicks Urijah just above the knee. Once, twice, and the third time Faber winces in pain, then smirks: *Thank you, sir, may I have another?* The Brazilian obliges, over and over serving up that brutal dessert with *Matrix*-like speed and precision.

How effective was this strategy? Well, by the end of the third round Faber's muay Thai coach, Master Thong, entered the cage and physically carried Faber back to the stool. It's a testament to Faber's ferocious will that he survived the five-round title bout.

"I was in a lot of pain, man," Urijah said the next day during an interview, propped on crutches while speaking into the camera. "From the second, middle-end of the second round . . . it was like, it was pretty painful in my legs. His leg kicks are deceiving. Feels like I was getting hit with a bat. First time I've ever been punished with those."

Urijah is smiling, but in his brief pauses it's clear he's awed by the power of those blows. "He caught me with a couple [leg kicks] in the first round. Like three, and they were starting to accumulate. I think he caught me with like seven in the second round. I'm not sure exactly when, but I went back to the corner and it looked like I had softballs on my—it was all lumped up on my leg, so . . . I was immobile after that. I couldn't really get spring. I was just kind of pushing through it."

Urijah pulls up his surf shorts and chuckles. "You can kind of see, here"—revealing his purplish thigh—"my leg matches my shorts."

The cameraman cannot contain his revulsion. "Oh my God, look at that," he moans. "Jesus, look at that bruise."

"Yeah, my leg's like twice the size of the other."

And Urijah is not exaggerating: his left thigh appears swollen and diseased. No wonder he's on crutches. "Even after the [post-fight] interview I felt like I was gonna pass out . . . I've never really felt like that before."

It's not mere muscle trauma that causes that body-core sickness but repeated strikes to the sciatic nerve.

Elbows

The elbow is ultra-effective in the clinch or on the ground, where there's no distance for a kick or a punch. With just a few inches of air a fighter can swing and deliver an unfathomable amount of power.

Jon Jones is the undisputed master of elbows. Held in closed guard, he lays an arm on his opponent's shoulder, baiting him to grab the wrist for control. *Jeez, I'm so tired, go ahead, it's yours.* Soon as fingers encircle the wrist he lifts the elbow and, pivoting off his opponent's grip like a fulcrum, drops an elbow onto the face.

Knees

There's no more dangerous position than the muay Thai clinch. Often initiated against the cage, a fighter grabs his opponent's neck with one hand, then the other, and lacing fingers behind the neck he jams elbows against the chest to control the distance, then yanks the head down while driving a knee into the solar plexus or chin. It's a textbook example of kinetic energy: the mass (*m*) of two bodies colliding at velocity (*v*). Now whether you grock the variables or not, it's easy to appreciate our opponent crumpling to the canvas. For a textbook example of this strategy, rewatch the *UFC 64* bout in which Anderson Silva, the challenger, grabbed Rich Franklin, the champion, by the neck, and for three straight minutes held tight and delivered knee after knee until Franklin dropped. TKO, 2:59 of the first round.

Most sensational is the flying knee. Needing to close distance, center of the ring a fighter hunches, leans forward, and jumps sometimes the length of his body. Mid-air the legs scissor, the chest bows out, and he delivers a knee with incredible force.

BOXING

After Royce Gracie so handily defeated Art "One Glove" Jimmerson in the inaugural UFC tournament, many armchair analysts, me included, felt boxing had no place in the cage. But I was wrong, again. In the ensuing years, numerous elite fighters have proven that incorporating boxing—the classic footwork, sliding head movements, punching angles—into a total MMA package nets a tremendous advantage.

Junior dos Santos, former UFC heavyweight champion, is renowned for his boxing prowess. Despite holding a brown belt in jiu-jitsu, Junior favors dropping overhand bombs, and at six-foot-four and 240 pounds, he believes he can stand to toe to toe with either of boxing's world-champion Klitschko brothers. "I wanna have a boxing fight one day, just to test me," he said prior to *UFC 146* in May 2012. "I used to train a lot of boxing. I'm a boxing guy. This could be a good challenge for me [to fight a Klitschko] . . . give [me] three months of preparation and I can fight anyone in the world, doesn't matter the sport, boxing or MMA."

Jason Parillo coaches numerous professional boxers as well as several MMA fighters, including Vitor Belfort, Tito Ortiz, and B.J. Penn. Backstage before the *UFC 152* weigh-ins in September 2012, I asked him the differences between muay Thai and boxing punches.

"Muay Thai fighters stand face to face and exchange, but boxers, they're stepping laterally, ducking to change levels, all while staying in the pocket—"

The pocket?

"That's what separates boxing from other [combat disciplines], the pocket. A boxer will stand inches from his opponent, and when a punch comes he ducks, weaves,

Jason Parillo holding mitts for B.J. Penn.

drops a shoulder, and avoids the blow. Then, *boom!,* delivers a counter[-punch]. It's all angles."

Angles?

"Okay, that's probably the most misunderstood term in boxing. When you hear the world *angle,* most people think footwork, stepping this way and that, cutting off the cage, but that's only one aspect. It also means shifting the shoulders a few inches, the head, the hips, the knees. These subtle movements allow boxers to stand in the pocket, avoid and deflect punches, then *boom!*"

I keep hearing about dirty boxing—why?

"The clinch, that's when fighters exchange in the clinch. Tying up arms, bumping with shoulders, grinding with the head."

Ah, that fighting against the cage . . . so who are the best boxers in MMA?

"Junior [dos Santos] is unreal. His hand speed, power—"

You think he could actually challenge Klitschko?

Jason laughs. "No disrespect, Junior is an unbelievable boxer, but that's like saying [boxer Floyd] Mayweather is gonna enter a jiu-jitsu tournament and beat Rafael Mendes [three-time jiu-jitsu world champion]. Not gonna happen. He might be the best MMA boxer, but that doesn't qualify him for the highest ranks of another sport. And boxing *is* another sport."

He's dropped other MMA fighters in seconds, so why not?

"Yeah, he's got power, but in a boxing match you're not worried about kicks, elbows, and takedowns. All the Klitschkos train is boxing, so they'd stand before him—in that pocket—and slip his punches. MMA fighters in the pocket are more flinchy because that next blow could come from anywhere. No, he would be outclassed. No disrespect."

How does boxing fit into an MMA fight strategy?

"It's front line because without throwing punches [MMA is] just a Pancrase match with guys slapping each other. And it's not just about striking or dodging blows. I teach fighters to judge distance with their jabs, and to control that distance with footwork. Miss and pay, miss and pay. You want your opponent to miss, then make him pay. That's what boxing is all about."

Is it different training boxers, as opposed to MMA fighters?

"Yes. With both you work on the mind-body connection, so those reactions are instant—slip and counter, slip and counter. The problem is MMA guys don't like to wear headgear, and that gear allows them to sit in the pocket, get comfortable while they're slipping punches. It allows them to train that instinct to flinch."

Any other great MMA boxers?

Jason scanned the fighters in line for the weigh-in, and seeing none of interest he rubbed his chin. "The Diaz brothers," he finally said. "They're good—*really* good. Nick spars with professional boxers, and I think he's had a few bouts."

So could he challenge at the pro boxing level?

"Doubt it. With that style he'd take a lot of damage. Like I said, it's so different when you're not worried about knees and kicks. But in the cage, those two [Nick and Nate] are dangerous."

—

On May 5, 2012, the circus rolled into East Rutherford, New Jersey, for *UFC on Fox 3.* Oh, and what a great night of boxing it would be: Nate Diaz was slated to face Jim Miller during the main bout, and minutes after the post-fight media scrum, Floyd Mayweather Jr. was squaring off with Miguel Cotto back in Vegas. We entered Dana's backstage dressing room just as the IT engineers finished wiring a flat-screen to carry the PPV stream.

Dana always loved boxing. When we were teens, I'd watch him and Artie Garrelli, another friend, pore over the betting lines, comparing fighters like horses: *he's got no legs . . . eight rounds, that dude'll gas . . . you're an idiot, his hands are soft . . . ah, he's got no chin . . .*

Nate Diaz warming up backstage.

My freshman year at the University of Nevada, Las Vegas (UNLV), we'd gather at our friend Marty Cordova's apartment, down beers, and scream at the television while playing *Rocky* on the Sega gaming console. And if Mike Tyson was fighting, well, we couldn't afford tickets for the actual bout, but we'd sneak into a bar or crash a party carrying the stream.

Dana left Vegas before my sophomore year at UNLV, and settling in Boston he took this boxing passion to the next level. He found a trainer and put in the hours working the bags, the mitts, learning footwork. For the first time in his life he found a calling and even fought a few amateur bouts.

Minutes before the *UFC on Fox 3* weigh-in, I run into Nick Diaz backstage. I'm pumped on the night's events, so I quiz him on Mayweather's dirty boxing, like how after a punch he lays his left forearm on an opponent's neck and, grappler-like, pushes off and even blocks blows. Nick mumbles something I don't quite get, then he searches the ground and wanders off.

Uh, okay.

No offense taken. Welcome to the world of Nick Diaz. Five times over the past year I've tried engaging him, and five times he ignored my comments and beelined for the exit. Nothing personal. Prior to his long-sought welterweight title bout with champion Georges St-Pierre at *UFC 137* in October 2011, he blew off a series of pre-fight press conferences. And when I say *blew off*, I mean he straight up went MIA. Fiasco doesn't come close to describing the ordeal. UFC *needs* fighters to promote bouts. That's the game. Fighters host media interviews, pressers, open workouts. So these no-shows sabotaged not only Nick's fight but also the entire *UFC 137* card.

After the second vanishing act Dana hit the roof and yanked away the brass ring. "I'd had my reservations about

The Diaz brothers: gameface.

Nick Diaz for a long time," he said at a later press conference. "You've heard me use the term 'play the game.' All I asked him for was *this* much. When he signed, I said, 'Let me tell you what, kid, add up all the purses of your career, this will be biggest fight of your life.' You have the opportunity to fight GSP and win the welterweight title. But I need you to do certain things."

St-Pierre chimed in: "I just don't understand why someone doesn't show up to an opportunity like this. Just can't believe it. It's amazing. It's crazy."

Crazy.

"He was going to make life-changing money for this fight," Dana said. "And maybe the thing is with Nick Diaz, maybe he did crack under the pressure. Maybe he folded under the spotlight."

A few days later Nick posted a response on YouTube: "Sorry I didn't make it to the beauty pageant . . . but, um, you know, I've never not showed up to a fight . . . I've never backed out of a fight in my life."

Not quite an apology, but that's Nick Diaz.

(Diaz was pulled from the card, but later fought, and lost to, GSP at *UFC 158*.)

Anyhow, enough about the elusive brother. Nate is just now entering the Octagon for his *Fox 3* main bout, and I'm cageside, listening to the referee's instructions. Nick and the rest of Nate's camp post-up a few feet away. The ref yells, "Fight!" Nate stalks forward, cruises straight into Miller's low kick, a few punches, then he answers with that trademark jab. Nick leans on the cage's outer runway, watching his little brother's every move. And watching him watch I wonder if he's studied fighting's ancient history. Does he know of the Olympic Games in the Colosseum? Does he know of Theogenes, the greatest MMA fighter to ever live? He and Nate so pass for spawns of this bloodline: the knotted brows, the flattened noses, the cauliflower ears.

Nate is lankier than the stocky Miller, and he easily holds him off with the southpaw jab. Right after right in the face. Miller answers with a low leg kick, then wrestles Nate

against the cage, anything to close the distance. But even in the clinch Nate is wiry, hard to control.

Nick screams at Nate: "Attack, attack, motherfucker!"

Nate breaks free, slides laterally, and jabs, upping the pace, using that reach to keep Miller at bay. He circles and cuts off the canvas, rat-a-tat-tatting that glove until Miller is blinking, ducking—anything but more sweaty leather in the eyes. During a clinch Nate ties Miller's arms and throws uppercuts—gut, gut, chin—using that dirty boxing to outstrike Miller 3:1.

End of the first round Nate throws a jab and follows with a straight left, crushing Miller's face and dropping him to the canvas.

Pace. Though Nate rocked Miller with a bomb, the knockdown wasn't just the result of a hard blow, it was due to the ever-increasing pace. *Pace* is the tried-and-true Diaz weapon. It's not their black belts in jiu-jitsu, their deadly accuracy, or their muay Thai knees. It's their relentless *pace.* Coming and coming deep into rounds when most fighters hang back, trying to regroup. Pace is why the brothers regularly compete in triathlons, honing their conditioning outside the gym—running, biking, swimming.

"Competing against the clock is the only way to tell you're improving," Nick told me. "Otherwise it's up to your trainer's best guess. Uh, yeah, you're sparring better than yesterday—what the fuck is that? Shit. A guy steps in that cage, you see whether he's put in the work. Looks great during a fight, well, that's 'cause he worked his ass off. Dude looks bad, he slacked."

In the second round Miller tries to slip the jabs, but he's eating leather. Nate senses desperation, raises his hands to taunt Miller, then slaps his own face. *What'choo got, bitch?* Miller leaps with a flying knee. Nate blocks with elbows, answers with a jab, hook, jab—a cat battering an

Ever the boxer, Junior Dos Santos in Academia Champion, the gym of famed trainer Luiz Carlos Dorea, Salvador, Bahia, Brazil. *(Credit: James Law)*

TEAM LUIZ DÓREA

ACADEMIA

CHAMPION

DESDE 1990

Jogos Sul-americanos - Ervan Conceição -Ouro, Alessandro Matos - Prata (02),
Adriana Araújo - Ouro, Erica Matos - Ouro, Everton Lopes - Prata (10)

exhausted mouse. Only in this nightmare the cat draws blood while ridiculing the mouse, which is another Diaz tactic: *head games.*

During *UFC 94* in January 2009, Clay Guida endured the Diaz (Nick) taunts. In a *Fight!* magazine interview later that year, he recalled, "He was sort of on my back near the cage and he kept yelling, '209, bitch! 209, bitch!' and I looked up and there was like 3:12 left on the clock. Later on I said to my coach, 'Dude, this guy can't even tell time! He kept yelling, '209, Bitch!' Then he told me that 209 is Stockton, California's area code—not the time left on the clock! I had to laugh."

Nate again raises both hands, mocking Miller. *Where you going?!* Which really means: *That's it, I'm done playing.* Nate throws Miller against the cage, dishes punch after punch. Miller shoots a half-ass double leg—*Just stop this, please.* Nate sprawls, wraps an arm around Miller's neck, rolls him into a guillotine, and chokes until Miller goes red-faced and taps, his first time ever.

Nick scrambles up the Octagon steps and grips the cage, and when the gate opens he hugs his swollen-faced little brother in a touching family scene straight out of *American Horror Story.*

After the post-fight media scrum, we rush into the dressing room and once again huddle around the TV—only this time not for video games but the Mayweather bout. The couches fill and Nick Diaz crams in beside me. As the fight progresses I comment on how in close quarters Mayweather keeps raising his left elbow to block Cotto, and I mention this because Nate pulled a similar move on Miller.

"Yeah, Mayweather's slick like that," Nick says, then mentions Mayweather's slap hook. "Watch Cotto step inside the pocket. Right there, Mayweather throws that quick left to the head."

What about muay Thai? I thought it was better suited to MMA than boxing, it's more brutal, more—

"Fucking kickboxers stand upright." Nick scowls. "Hands here [illustrating hands alongside temples], moving straight forward. That shit's predictable. But boxing, I'm coming at you more [crouched] like a wrestler, backing you up with jabs. I see an opening, I can shoot a takedown without really changing levels."

But if I guy's throwing kicks, like José Aldo, how does boxing help with that?

"Fuck muay Thai. How you gonna kick me when I'm backing you into the cage with my jab? Boxing's where it's at."

Translation: If you're ever in a fight with Nick Diaz, and he's coming and coming with that ruthless jab, too close to kick, shoot a double-leg or count yourself fucked.

WRESTLING

A fourteen-year-old wrestler runs the dirt roads near his home, mile after mile, on through sunrise. He lifts iron, trains with teammates, and starves himself every week to make weight, all in hopes of winning a state championship, competing for his favorite college, and perhaps climbing that Olympic podium. (As of this writing, wrestling is in jeopardy as an Olympic sport. The UFC is working with the International Wrestling Federation for the reinstatement of the sport at the 2020 Olympic Games.) But that's the end of the rainbow. Not even a hope of financial compensation beyond coaching.

Yet the UFC explosion has changed this kid's dreams. MMA coaches now scout collegiate tournaments for potential recruits. *Why?* Because wrestling is the perfect minor leagues for MMA. Wrestlers endure grueling three-hour practices of non-stop conditioning; drilling moves, sparring, usually while dehydrated and starving to make weight for that week's match or tournament. And glory? Wrestling sits on the lowest shelf compared with football, basketball,

Johny Hendricks in New York City.

baseball, and soccer. Most girls are repulsed by thoughts of sweaty guys in leotards rolling on ringworm-infected mats. No empirical data here (just my own experience as both a high school wrestler and football player), but scan the bleachers at any wrestling match and you'll see the lowest girl-to-athlete ratio of any sport, save, I don't know, maybe bowling, or badminton. But this unloved sport translates perfectly to MMA.

"Wrestling is basically a simulated fight with certain rules," Urijah Faber told me. "It's about imposing your will on somebody, holding the guy down, and putting him in a position he does not want. And that's what fighting is about."

Wrestlers are grinders; thus, they easily slide into the grueling training sessions required of MMA. No balking at the countless hours required to learn muay Thai, jiu-jitsu, boxing. Also, having competed in weekly matches and multi-day tournaments for most of their lives, wrestlers enter the Octagon less prone to the backstage adrenaline spike-and-dump that leaves many inexperienced fighters sapped just as they enter the cage. That's no small thing, as managing nerves is a big part of the fight game.

Johny Hendricks, two-time Division I National Wrestling Champion and UFC welterweight contender, told me: "By the time I first [fought MMA] I'd competed thousands of times. And wrestling in college, that's the elite level—the pressure is enormous, but you learn to tune all that out: the crowds, the expectations. So I don't get nervous before a fight, not even during the walkout. I'm just there to enjoy the experience."

But more than a Sun Tzu mindset, there's a style advantage to wrestling. A wrestler's low, explosive stance enables him to shoot and, *like that*, penetrate a striker's radius—*yeah, I saw you 'bout to throw that overhand right, but here's what I'm thinking we do*—and with that our wrestler wraps and slams him to the mat. Now the fun begins. Crushing an opponent against the cage, snatching legs, ground-and-pound, and, of course, takedown defense are all critical elements of an effective fight plan, and each requires wrestling skills.

That's why so many college wrestlers populate the MMA history books: Chuck Liddell, Randy Couture, Tito Ortiz, Cain Velasquez, Ben Askren, Rashad Evans, Chael Sonnen, Matt Hughes, Matt Hamill, Johny Hendricks, Quinton "Rampage" Jackson, Chad Mendes, Gray Maynard, Matt Lindland, Joseph Benavidez, Shane Carwin, Brock Lesnar, Jon Fitch, Urijah Faber, and so on.

And the wrestling takeover is only just beginning. Hear that rumbling in the fields? That's the wrestling masses coming for this newfound fame and cash. According to berecruited.com, every year in the United States alone, roughly 260,000 wrestlers compete in club, high school, and college meets; and for these up-and-comers the path from wrestling to mixed martial arts is the new Yellow Brick Road. That's why the leading annual MMA conventions—the UFC Fan Expo and the Fight Summit Industry Conference—feature not only vendor booths and seminars but also prestigious wrestling tournaments.

Irony of ironies, one of the greatest wrestlers in MMA never wrestled in high school or college. Georges St-Pierre, the current welterweight champion, tested his mat skills at *UFC 74* in August 2007 when he faced famed wrestler Josh Koscheck, four-time Division I All-American, who, during his junior year at Edinboro University, smoked forty-two straight opponents, never losing once, en route to winning the National Championships.

It was a tough fight to predict: GSP had just lost his belt to Matt Sera, while Koscheck was charging through the ranks, screaming for a title shot. Handicappers gave GSP the striking advantage, but they questioned whether he could withstand Koscheck's grappling. Wrestler versus striker, a classic matchup. Let's cue up the bout: Octagon announcer Bruce Buffer introduces the fighters. The crowd roars. The ref starts the action, and after circling a bit Koscheck jabs and whiffs an overhand right, jabs, jabs and whiffs another

Josh Koscheck warms up backstage.

overhand right, while GSP backs away and throws a half-hearted kick. Just what you expected, until the script flips and Koscheck kicks and GSP counters with a pristine double-leg takedown. Cheers erupt. Joe Rogan, calling the action, quips, "Whoa, good takedown," and he seems just as surprised as Koscheck. From then on GSP outwrestles Koscheck fence to fence, at times rag-dolling the grappling standout and earning a unanimous decision.

"I didn't believe he could possibly take me down," Koscheck said in an MMAweekly.com interview after the loss. "I didn't think that was an option. Throughout camp my mental game was work on my stand-up, work on my stand-up, because this guy isn't going to be able to take me down. . . that's something I've learned over the past couple of years, it's just not wrestling, I gotta become a complete fighter."

There it is. GSP proved a fighter can master wrestling skills much later in life. An hour before his walkout at *UFC 154* in November 2012, as GSP lays out his *gi*, he tells me: "I wrestle four hours a week. Karate I don't train so much, it's more incorporating specific techniques into my regimen. But wrestling I still work on nearly every day."

That's impressive, as wrestling practice sucks. Nothing I've done compares—not football, not jiu-jitsu. Nothing. As I've never trained for an MMA fight, I asked Josh Koscheck if that's the case.

How does wrestling prepare a fighter for career in MMA?

"Ground-up wrestling, competing at the highest one-on-one level for twenty years, makes you a man. Wrestling is the hardest sport in the world when it comes to training and competing. I've never put my body through workouts like wrestling workouts."

Why is wrestling so effective in MMA?

"Wrestling is the *best sport* for MMA because [wrestling provides] the foundation for controlling where the fight takes place. If you have the ability to take the fight to the ground, and keep it there, you will most likely win the fight."

So you still train straight wrestling?

"Yes, we train wrestling one day a week. And during every sparring session we wrestle."

Was it difficult to transition from wrestling to MMA?

"Not really. The biggest transition was learning to put everything together."

How does MMA training compare, intensity-wise, to wrestling?

"Pure wrestling is way harder. Not even a comparison. If I was to only train for a wrestling match, that's a son of a bitch. Not that MMA training isn't hard, but straight wrestling training is nuts. You put in so much work, and the only reward is getting your hand raised at the end of the match. MMA training is also hard, and sometimes I ask myself what the hell I'm doing, but the reward is much sweeter. You get your hand raised, *and* you get paid."

TRADITIONAL MARTIAL ARTS

It's 1973—the year of bell-bottoms, brown acid, and war protests. Riots in the streets. *Enter the Dragon* dropped in theaters, and across the country hippie kids staggered from double doors arguing whether Bruce Lee was indeed the baddest motherfucker ever to walk the earth.

This wasn't just another Hong Kong flick; this was a culture bomb whose fallout still radiates today. Take the film's opening fight: Lee circles his opponent wearing MMA-style kenpo gloves and modern fight shorts, they tangle, Lee throws him several times, fairly typical fight choreography, but then drops on his downed challenger and wrenches an armbar for the submission.

Ask any UFC fighter to name the most influential kung fu legend and no doubt nine out of ten will reply "Bruce Lee."

Even Manny Pacquiao, world champion boxer, idolized the master. "Bruce Lee was a big influence on me," Pacquiao said in a Yahoo! Sports interview. "The first movie I saw was *Enter the Dragon*, when I was 8. Every time we'd leave the movie theater after one of his movies, we'd all jump around and kick. In my early years [as a fighter], I tried to emulate his style in terms of speed and quickness. And I still do a little now."

If you haven't seen the film, set this book down and cue up a copy. Now skip to the climactic fight scene where Lee, cat-like, enters the room of mirrors, slinking past his own muscled reflections. Those black pants and clenched fists. That scowl—

Press Pause. In the background cue up Wu-Tang Clan, light some incense, and press Play.

Lee stalks through the room while Shih Kien sneaks behind him, that steel Wolverine claw locked and loaded. Lee turns the corner and Kien is everywhere at once. Lee rubbernecks this way and that, swings and misses, for a moment lost in the surreal mind-trip.

Taoism teaches that the world is a series of illusions, which acolytes must shatter to find Nirvana. Lee knows this. He exhales, goes zen, and punches a mirror, then another and another, each smash negating Kien's advantage. Revealing the real and forcing Kien into the open. Lee smirks, throws a side kick into Kien's solar plexus, and launches him across the room, impaling him on a spear.

That's how a revolution takes root. *Enter the Dragon* inspired kids across America to seek out and join neighborhood dojos, and traditional martial arts (TMA) flourished: kenpo, tae kwon do, shotokan, aikido—like religion these disciplines infected American culture, spreading throughout the 1970s and 1980s. Fly to Vegas and two shows a night you could watch Elvis, draped in bedazzled jumpsuits, performing his kata on a casino showroom stage. And how about Van Halen's "Panama" video, with David Lee Roth swinging that Japanese sword while kicking whirlwinds?

TMA ruled the land. According to *Tae Kwon Do: The Ultimate Reference Guide to the World's Most Popular Martial Art* (1989), by the late 1980s, tae kwon do boasted more practitioners than any other self-defense system. That is until *Gracie Jiu-Jitsu in Action*, followed by the inaugural UFC tournament. In very public displays these events ripped the veil from TMA, exposing their weaknesses against other styles. During those early UFCs both Ken Shamrock and Royce Gracie made quick work of Patrick Smith, a black belt in hapkido, kenpo, tae kwon do, and tang soo do. And how about *UFC 11.5* and Tank Abbott's brutal KO of karate maven Steve Nelmark?

Joe Rogan, ringside commentator for the UFC, trained tae kwon do throughout his teens, and eventually earned a second dan black belt and won the 1987 tae kwon do U.S. Open Championships. "Every young kid thinks his art is perfect," he told me, "but after a few years you spar against other styles and it's like, 'Oh shit, what's wrong here, there's so many holes in my game.' That's when I started training muay Thai."

Fast-forward two decades. You'd think TMA would have vanished from the scene, but stroll into any MMA gym and you'll find fighters practicing wheel kicks, roundhouse kicks—channeling that old-school Bruce Lee. As with most other disciplines, MMA fighters seek to incorporate TMA's most effective elements.

And that's a good thing because those traditional kicks deliver far and away the most memorable highlights in MMA: Lyoto Machida's crane kick that dropped Randy Couture at *UFC 129* in April 2011; Anderson Silva's front kick that disposed of Vitor Belfort at *UFC 126* in February 2011; Edson Barboza's spinning wheel kick that nearly flatlined Terry Etim at *UFC 142* in January 2012; Vitor Belfort dropping Luke Rockhold with a spinning heel kick at *UFC on Fox 8*; Junior Dos Santos catching Mark Hunt with a wheel kick at *UFC 160*; and how about Anthony Pettis running *Matrix*-style along the cage, then slamming his foot into Benson Henderson's jaw at *WEC 53* in December 2010.

But how powerful are these TMA strikes versus other styles? *National Geographic* explored this very question in *Fight Science*, a mini-documentary evaluating the biomechanical force of blows from various disciplines. In a high-tech warehouse, engineers rigged computers, cameras, sensors, pads, heavy bags—everything needed to measure

velocity and power. Four martial arts masters lined the stage, eager to demonstrate their most powerful weapons. A capoeira kick took the early lead, clocking in at 99 mph and 1,800 pounds of force. The muay Thai kick clocked in at 130 mph, but only delivered 1,400 pounds of force. Last came the tae kwon do kick, which stole the crown with a jaw-dropping 136 mph and 2,300 pounds of force.

"It takes ten years to master those kicks," Rogan continued, "and by that time, not many [traditional] fighters want to start pursuing other disciplines. But I think once guys realize, you'll see those kicks incorporated more and more—take the axe kick, that's one of the best in the game."

Rogan knows what he's talking about. In an infamous YouTube video he teaches GSP to correctly throw a spinning back kick, a staple from his heyday. In the clip, Joe steps at the heavy bag, spins, and unleashes a waist-level kick that nearly unchains the bag. "Man, that's fucking crazy," GSP mutters.

While TMA is not the most-trodden route into the cage, numerous elite MMA fighters hold the pedigree: GSP, Lyoto Machida, Stephen Thompson, Gunnar Nelson, Cung Le, Daron Cruickshank, and Edson Barboza, to name a few. Oh, and let's not forget Anderson Silva, who walks into the arena with Steven Seagal, the biggest 1980s TMA film star and practitioner.

Prior to Montreal's *UFC 154* weigh-in in November 2012, I sat with Lyoto Machida—a fan favorite due to his unorthodox karate-based fighting style—and quizzed him on his training. Machida's father started him in shotokan karate at just four years old. Shotokan philosophy flows from ancient Bushido precepts, a.k.a. samurai, and stresses honor, courage, respect, and loyalty. Shotokan's founder, Gichin Funakoshi, taught students that "the ultimate aim of Karate lies not in victory or defeat, but in the perfection of the character of the participant." Like Helio Gracie,

Lyoto Machida, the Dragon.

Master Funakoshi was frail and timid, and he developed the discipline to compensate for these deficiencies.

Do you think karate is still as viable a path into MMA today as it was when you started?

"I think it is very important to learn the fundaments of each martial art. Especially when you are a kid . . . not only the principles but also the philosophy of each martial art. [That is why a fighter] should come up through a particular discipline, and not just the MMA approach."

What aspects of karate apply to MMA?

"Throughout its evolution karate lost itself. [That's why] I look to the fundamentals, to karate's roots, [which emphasized] the knees, kicks, and elbows."

Like muay Thai?

"Yes."

Did you compete in karate tournaments?

"Many times, and this helped [with] nerves, emotions—and also technique because the footwork you learn from competing, it's different from the gym."

Which [TMA] kicks work best in MMA?

"The front kick." [I wonder, as Lyoto stares at the ground and chuckles, whether he's reliving the *Karate Kid* kick he unleashed to knock Randy Couture's tooth across the mat.] "Also the spinning back kick, and the wheel kick."

After karate, what did you train?

"Sumo. Then jiu-jitsu, since I was fifteen."

How did you develop your fists?

"When I first started my fighting career I went to Bangkok and trained muay Thai. But no matter what else I trained, I always incorporated it into karate. My fighting style comes from karate. I have incorporated other styles, but it's still karate. I learn from everything, even old karate books."

What do you think about Bruce Lee?

"Ah, great fighter, great actor. A legend."

How about the martial art that Lee innovated, Jeet Kune Do?

"A visionary, a true martial artist. He used everything. Really, he invented MMA years ago."

What karate philosophy most guides you as a fighter?

"Peace. Before a fight I empty my mind. Every fighter is able to lose. It is not a big thing. You have to accept what comes and remain calm."

When you're fighting for a championship bout, how do you find that peace with so much on the line?

"You just look at it naturally—this is all part of nature. Accept, and believe in yourself: that's the main thing. There is always the internal pressure, and also the pressure from fans, the organization, media. You just have to eliminate as much as you can."

Which discipline do you feel provides the best path into MMA—karate, muay Thai, wrestling, or boxing?

"I have never trained as a pure artist in other modalities, so I wouldn't know."

Per week, how much time do you spend training karate?

"I am always training karate. In every moment, whether walking down the sidewalk, standing in line. Sometimes, just waiting for a green light I will visualize different fight situations. This is all part of my training."

MMA

All this discourse brings us back to that age-old question: Which style rules the cage?

Jiu-jitsu?

Muay Thai?

Wrestling . . . Boxing . . . Tae kwon do . . . Kalarippayattu . . . Aikido . . . Shotokan . . . Savate . . . Tinku . . . Capoeira . . . Lucha Libre . . . Kenpo . . . Bok Fu . . . Shootfighting . . . Sli Beatha . . . Kajukenbo . . . Bojuka . . . Wen-Do . . . Sarit Sarak . . . Thang-Ta . . . Gatka . . . Silat . . . Judo . . . Sumo . . . Kumdo . . . Subak . . . Yusul . . . Bando . . . Dumog . . . Yaw-Yan . . . Nhat Nam . . . Pankration . . . Glima . . . Nova Scrimia . . . Sambo . . . Krav Maga . . . Mau Rakau . . . Buno . . .

In the end, Bruce Lee said it best:

If you want to understand the truth in martial arts, to see any opponent clearly, you must throw away the notion of styles or school, prejudices, likes and dislikes, and so forth. Then, your mind will cease all conflict and come to rest. In this silence, you will see totally and freshly.

Or better yet—the best style is *no* style.

If Lee were alive today, no doubt he'd counsel modern fighters to cherry-pick each discipline, select only techniques suited to the particular fighter's physiology, mental makeup, and existing game. If a great muay Thai fighter faces a decent wrestler, what happens is the wrestler blocks that infamous leg kick and charges the kickboxer against the cage, slams and ground and pounds his face bloody. KO. But teach that kickboxer to sprawl and shuck a mean crossface—that's a lethal combination. That's José Aldo. That's Anderson Silva.

Teach a world-class wrestler boxing footwork and how to throw a devastating Rocky Marciano–style overhand right? That's Dan Henderson unleashing his patented H-bomb. Or Johny Hendricks dropping foes in thirty seconds.

Teach a jiu-jitsu practitioner muay Thai—you get it, a modern MMA fighter *must* diversify.

SKILLS VERSUS PATH

So all these diverse skills are vital to a fight plan, but what's the surest path into the cage?

Initially, viewing the landscape from under the long shadow cast by Royce Gracie, I assumed jiu-jitsu provided the golden route. Then, from casual observations and barroom discussions, I assumed muay Thai. But it wasn't until I graphed the stats that I saw the real map.

In categorizing each fighter, based on available information (website bios, interviews), I determined each fighter's initial combat discipline—for example, if a fighter started tae kwon do at age nine, and added jiu-jitsu at seventeen, then that fighter was primarily shaped by tae kwon do. Why? Because fresh off the street a kid is malleable, a tabula rasa quickly programmed with that discipline's techniques, philosophies, work ethic. Subsequent training in other disciplines doesn't erase that foundation, it merely builds upon it. Sifting through the information, I was forced to make a few subjective calls—such as, does a year of kung fu followed by five years of wrestling define a fighter's foundation as TMA or wrestling (I'd argue TMA, if he/she continued with kung fu)—but how empirical can we get with qualifiers such as *primary influence?*

Of the roughly 349 UFC active fighters under contract, 120 started in wrestling. That's nearly twice any other discipline. I was most shocked that muay Thai trailed TMA. Perhaps it's an era thing, and given time muay Thai's popularity will draft the expansion of MMA. Or perhaps it's an institutional thing, due to the countless tae kwon do gyms still anchoring strip malls around the world, and in coming years we'll this see less and less. Time will tell.

There it is. No matter the race for second, third, and fourth, there's no question that wrestling far and away leads the pack.

THE NEW BREED

But hold up, before signing your youngster into the local wrestling program, think, *Evolution.* Think, *A new option— the Sixth Option.*

As one of the first pure-MMA fighters to excel in the UFC, Rory MacDonald best represents this new breed. At just twenty years old he amassed a 10–0 record, starting anew the whispers of "phenom" and "future champion." So UFC matchmaker Joe Silva pitted him against elite veteran Carlos Condit for *UFC 115* in June 2010. Only his second big-show outing, "career test" doesn't begin to describe the bout. Yet Rory manhandled Condit, outstriking,

outwrestling, putting on a veritable MMA clinic through the first two rounds, hands down securing the decision. Then, middle of the third and final round, Rory dropped his head and panted for air, losing steam. Condit turned on the attack: after slamming the kid he dropped relentless elbows—fracturing Rory's orbital, breaking his nose, and, *like that,* the momentum flipped, and with just ten seconds remaining the ref stepped in, waving his hands.

A heartbreaker, if ever. Ten seconds. *If* Rory could have just stymied the attack for ten more clicks he would have emerged with a perfect record and probably a shot at the belt.

If only. So goes MMA: count no victory until the bell sounds.

Rory and I ate breakfast together in Toronto, and wolfing down two plates of eggs and pancakes he shrugged off the loss, as though it was a perfect stepping stone toward his eventual title. We talked training, head games, and his path into the cage.

"I was pretty lucky to find a good MMA gym in a small town ten years ago," Rory said. "Ten years ago a good MMA gym was pretty hard to come by. I guess I was one of the first [pure MMA fighters] that's in the UFC now. But I think you'll see more and more of it with the growth of the sport, the popularity. So many young kids want to get into it."

How is this evolution going to effect the sport?

"I think [new fighters] will have a lot more balanced style. There's no longer going to be one-specialty fighters. I think those guys are gonna get weeded out pretty fast. Now you have to be balanced in every discipline to make it in the UFC."

How did you find the gym?

"My dad and brother and I were in the car, and my brother was saying he went to a class at an MMA gym. We'd been watching UFC since I was little. So we got all excited talking about it, and my dad was like, 'So do you wanna go?' I said yeah, and right then he turned the car around. I did a

class and fell in love. . . it was a no-*gi* jiu-jitsu class and a bit of striking. The gym was grimy, but so badass. We hit the heavy bag, shadowboxing, and some MMA on the ground, and I was hooked. I told my dad when I got in the car, this is what I'm doing, this is it, I am quitting hockey and all that shit."

What did he say?

"He was down 'cause it was way cheaper!"

So the more holistic foundation of pure MMA helps, as opposed to coming up through another discipline?

"Yeah, because your thinking is always geared toward an MMA fight. If your outlook is coming from a muay Thai background, then you're always thinking stand-up. Jiu-jitsu, the ground. My outlook is always to mix it up and change at any moment. So starting young in an MMA gym is ideal, in my opinion."

THE CAGE

It's hard to imagine that John Milius comprehended the true impact of introducing those eight vertical planes on the nascent sport. He'd trained jiu-jitsu with Rorion Gracie, but as a renowned Hollywood director he was no doubt more focused on the drama and symbolism of the cage: how, positioned under thousands of cheering fans, it emotes ancient combat, danger, sacrifice, and rebirth.

But the impact of those eight fences on fight strategy is immense.

Most combat plays out on a flat surface: the ref signals *Fight!* and you're projecting only along the *x-axis*—moving forward and back, sideways, cutting angles. Think merely in 2-D and you're good. But introduce four sides of loose ropes, like in boxing and muay Thai, and you can trap your opponent in the corner and rain blows or, in rare instances à la Muhammad Ali, lean on the top rope to exhaust your

Rory MacDonald, pure MMA.

opponent with the rope-a-dope. However these maneuvers require only minute calculations on the *y-axis*.

But throw a vinyl-coated fence around the horizontal and you'd better start mapping in 3-D. Ignore the cage and next thing it's against your back, restricting movement, and, oh yeah, how about that head under your chin, and the knee slamming your thigh, over and over until it cramps. There goes your fight strategy, at least until you get the hell off of there.

Here's the thing: I couldn't stand when fighters landed against the cage, swimming arms for underhooks, shoving and tugging. But as with jiu-jitsu, I was ignorant and needed a primer to understand. So I rapped with Chuck Liddell, watched hundreds of fights, and here's my take-away:

Cage Strategy #1: Basic Offense: Pin your opponent back against the chain-link, driving his shoulder into his chest, stepping your front leg between his, jam your head under his chin and stretch him out. This *stretch* weakens his base. Now clench his waist and slam him to the mat.

Cage Strategy #2: Basic Defense: When faced with #1, don't stand there like a dummy. Turn your hips, shift your feet parallel with the cage, swim your rear arm under his armpit, and pull higher, higher, until it's him now stretched and off balance. Now turn him 180 degrees against the cage and implement #1.

Cage Strategy #3: The Crab Back: If you find yourself taken down, crab your hands backward until you feel the cage at your shoulders, then perform a leg press against it and stand. Now start on #2.

Cage Strategy #4: The Escape: God forbid, if ever you're on your back fending off a submission, walk your legs up the chain-link and get vertical, thus reducing the torque on your arm/neck, and perhaps even escape.

Cage Strategy #5: The Holiday: A variant of #2, but instead of working for a reversal, just lean back and rest. B.J. Penn showed how, pinned against the cage, a fighter needn't panic. Maybe it's an Aloha thing, but he'd just chill there, letting his opponent burn through the gas tank. Once recharged, shift to #2.

Cage Strategy #6: The Corner: Backpedal into the cage to prevent a takedown. Sure, I can't sprawl when I'm against the fence, but you can't shoot a double leg. No room. Anderson Silva used this against Chael Sonnen during *UFC 151*, thus negating his wrestling.

Cage Strategy #7: The Diaz: What you do is throw relentless jabs while walking your opponent down, the whole time talking shit—*bitch, you want some of this? 209, motherfucker!*—and once his back hits the chain-link, jab, slap hook, left uppercut, then deep-slip his counter, and tackle him against the cage. Employ #1 for a bit, then break free and repeat #7.

All cage strategies employ risk management. Reduce the variables and you need only concentrate on what remains. Clinched against the fence you eliminate kicks, flying knees, spinning fists. Now you're only dealing with dirty boxing, knees, elbows, and takedowns.

Helio Gracie wanted to simulate a street fight. The grandmaster was a purist, and if he'd had his way, the UFC would've taken place behind a convenience store—with just a handful of onlookers, a flickering lamppost, and a camera to record the action. But life is full of compromises. Fans want to watch. Governments wants to regulate. In the end, modern MMA is the closest, on a worldwide scale, that we'll get to his vision.

Every principal discipline that comprises the sport—jiu-jitsu, wrestling, muay Thai, boxing—is shaped by the confines of their respective rules. Stringent rules. Yet, in the cage those rules vanish. Boxers must defend takedowns. Wrestlers must fend off head kicks. Jiu-jitsu players must block upper cuts. It's a beautiful calculus, in which subtraction yields a sport so new, so innovative, from here on its adherents will likely only train the sport itself. Welcome to the brave new world of MMA.

Lavar Johnson vs. Pat Barry.

4: THE HERO'S JOURNEY

SO HERE WE ARE, recounting history, dissecting styles and techniques, but in many ways this focus obscures the true source of every victory: *The Will*. And what I mean is, the immeasurable doggedness that drives a fighter to train through exhaustion and pain, to ignore thirst and hunger while shooting takedowns, hitting the mitts, to suppress the ego and work through awkward movements, honing kicks and footwork until they flow effortless.

None of which is easy. Some mornings a fighter wakes and stares at the empty ceiling, and in those cold, alone moments, to reassure himself he summons the chants and envisions his hand raised in the Octagon, until lying there he floats in that warm glow. The alarm buzzes, but just a few more minutes to stave off the doubt, and worse—the fear, yes, *fear*—because those shadows on the periphery are always there. Fear of failure, fear of pain, fear of career-ending injury and shame. A mirror glint and it creeps back, the light dimming to dark for just an instant, until again he summons this scene and convinces himself: *No, I got this, I am the fucking man!*

Welcome to martial arts, where the true battle unfolds within, where our innate dualities compete for attention: courage/fear, yin/yang.

In his seminal book *The Hero with a Thousand Faces*, author Joseph Campbell revealed the blueprint underlying all great stories: Sumerian myths, biblical parables, kung fu movies, and even *The Matrix*. Campbell leaned heavily on Carl Jung, looting his work on subconscious archetypes, and also on that nihilistic German sage Arthur Schopenhauer, whose seminal essays explored the human *will*; and thus, Campbell laid out "The Hero's Journey," a template that

Vitor Belfort suffering. *(Credit: Ryan Loco)*

features a broken character searching for redemption, encountering obstacles, until on the desolate road he meets a mentor, and battling inner demons he grows, is reborn, and, achieving victory, earns a treasure that helps, not only himself, but his people.

Campbell theorized the reason this same pattern occurs across continents, cultures, races, and religions is because inside, despite our differences, we're all made of the same hopes, the same fears, the same dreams. In one form or another, it's the journey we all face, so we need to hear/see the story over and over, just with different heroes, obstacles, and settings.

Flip through late-night TV movies and you'll see the pattern:

A young peasant endures a brutal beating at the hands of an evil warlord's minions, so he skulks into a monastery and meets an old man who sets him to peculiar, hellish tasks. The peasant questions, doubts, wants to quit training but sticks with it, and after arduous trials he emerges to conquer the warlord, and a hero is born.

If this sounds like a spiritual quest, well . . .

"It is always a battle of the spirits," Lyoto Machida told me in Montreal, "inside the Octagon, and out. It doesn't matter. Training every day, even when you are going to close a major [business] deal, it is a battle of the spirits."

That's why it's called mixed *martial arts*—despite how it looks, the sport is *not* merely about smashing and snapping—it's about that dawn-of-time mystical journey. The Hero's Journey.

TRAINING CAMP

Though an MMA fighter works out year-round, come eight weeks before a fight he enters camp. General training yields to increased intensity, focus on fight strategy, a monastic diet, and mental strain unlike anything, the days ticking away, millions watching, waiting.

"When I'm in camp, we make my opponent out as a monster," lightweight title contender Joe Lauzon told me. "We focus on his strengths because that's what we need to negate. Right off the bat, take away his tools. Find training partners who can simulate those strengths, then work on jamming him up and eliminating how he'll hurt you."

Training day in, day out, you arrive at the gym after breakfast, again after lunch, and, oh, let's head back before dinner, as if all this training won't kill the thrill and shatter the body. Split fingernail. Swollen cheek. Aching elbow. Still you hump along, leaving every sparring session wheezing for breath with these strained ribs, nose throbbing from the constant jabs, but don't complain because this is what you signed up for, and fuck if you don't need this fight.

"Boxing is a grind, I hate it because it's my weakness and I have to put so much time into [improving it]," Lauzon told me. "Getting punched in the face for an hour straight, that sucks. But rolling jiu-jitsu is my favorite. It completely picks me up. Even if I'm losing I have a good time. I'm serious when I say grappling brightens my week—to go for an awesome sweep or submission, even if I don't make it, who cares, I'm having fun."

Too bad this is MMA and not choose-the-discipline-you-like-best, for in the cage you gotta prepare all weapons, especially those needed in fifty-six, fifty-five, fifty-four days and counting. "When camp starts, we buckle down and start grinding it out," Steve Maze, Lauzon's striking coach, explained. "The first week we're just getting back into it, formulating a game plan, looking at different combinations. Everything is geared toward the opponent, because it doesn't make sense to work on things you're not going to use in the fight. I get the DVDs [of opponents' fights] from the UFC, then I make copies for all the coaches and sparring partners."

Old fight videos are key, not just for devising strategy but also for stoking the fire. "In MMA you're only as good as your last fight," Lauzon said, "so I like watching my old fights and seeing where I screwed up. Even Anderson Silva,

if he drops a few fights they'll start saying he's overrated, and he was never that good. That's just how it is. Fans are fickle. I've had some good fights, but when I drop the ball fans immediately tweet how bad I suck. That's the game. So I go back and watch old fights that didn't go so well, get ideas for things I should work that day."

Joe also watches other fighters for motivation, particularly his hero, Kazushi Sakuraba. In the early 2000s, Sakuraba earned the moniker "Gracie Hunter" after defeating Royce, Renzo, Royler, and Ryan Gracie. "I know his fights are old," Lauzon said, "but people still make highlights of the guy. It's so inspiring because even if he was losing, really getting his ass kicked, from nowhere he'd pull some crazy submission and win. He always thought outside the box; like, fuck typical tactics, because there's always another solution. I also watch B.J. Penn, the Diaz brothers—any guys that really go for it."

Coaches treat camp like a clock repair shop: each week they wind the spring tighter and tighter, in the hope that the coiled whiplash releases the night of the fight, causing maximum destruction. "You don't want your best day during camp," coach Maze said, "not that you should look terrible for eight weeks, but during that time you want to get beat up because if you're [besting] guys every time you spar or roll, then guess what, you don't have anything to work on and you're cheating yourself. During camp I want to break a fighter down, push him as hard as I can so if something goes wrong on fight night he can mentally push through it. The last thing you want is your boy's will to break during a fight. That's why every week we run Simulation Saturdays, where whatever he's gonna do day of the fight—take a shower, have breakfast—that's what he does, so it's routine. Then he spars for an hour straight, rotating out fresh guys to simulate the worst-case scenario."

To cope with the mental strain, after training Joe Lauzon, like many fighters, retreats into his cave for nightly sessions on the Xbox. "Playing video games helps me switch my mind off from training. If I make a mistake while

sparring, during dinner and lying in bed I'll obsess on it . . . you fucked up, you shouldn't have lowered your hand, why did you turn after that kick . . . it haunts me. Driving, eating, showering, it's still going through my brain. But *Call of Duty*, the constant strategizing, the I'm-gonna-die-if-I-don't-dive-into-that-hole, it forces my brain to switch over, and that keeps me sharp during camp."

DIET

What's he walk at?

It's one of the most important questions in MMA. *Why?* Because a fighter wants every available advantage: speed, strength, technique, *and* weight. So during camp he restricts meals and sheds every ounce of fat, then during fight week he cuts water and, stepping on the scale, let's say he makes weight at 170 pounds—well, that night he rehydrates, and after a few light meals to bulge the vacant intestinal tract, the next day he enters the cage weighing much, much more.

That's how Rory MacDonald rolls, and it proved an enormous advantage over B.J. Penn during their *UFC on Fox 5* bout in Seattle in December 2012. Unlike most fighters, throughout camp B.J. struggled to *gain* weight—who knows why, really—and after eight weeks—fully hydrated and bowels bulged—he tipped the official scales at 168. That's two pounds *under* the welterweight limit.

Now this doesn't sound like much, but on fight night B.J. entered the cage at 168, effectively handing Rory an enormous advantage. It's simple algebra, whether we're talking ten, fifteen, or however many extra pounds Rory packed behind every punch and every kick. This isn't a subjective

Joe Lauzon (center) with Steve Maze (left) and Ricky Lundell (right).

edge, it's hard physics: as in $P=MA*V$ (Power equals Mass Acceleration multiplied by Velocity). Jump to Chapter 6 for the outcome.

So there's the combat advantage, or at least a need to level the field, but denying the flesh also steels the mind and ups the chi—again, a spiritual thing. Great thinkers from Plato to Jesus have long advocated fasting and refusing the body, and it's perhaps the most divine trial a fighter faces. In the words of Henry David Thoreau: "Every man is the builder of a temple, called his body, to the god he worships, after a style purely his own, nor can he get off by hammering marble instead. We are all sculptors and painters, and our material is our own flesh and blood and bones."

Though we mere mortals might never throw a punch or drop an elbow, we've all denied ourselves a warm donut or an oven-fresh chocolate chip cookie—so it's no revelation that dieting sucks. The body wants what the body wants.

Mike Dolce, nutritionist to numerous UFC fighters, including Vitor Belfort and Chael Sonnen, cemented his reputation when he supervised Quinton "Rampage" Jackson's massive weight cut prior to his bout with Rashad Evans. It was a remarkable feat, especially given how Dolce spurns the traditional wrestler/boxer starvation approach. Instead, his fighters feast on fresh veggies, fruits, whole grains, coupled with small portions of grass-fed beef or wild fish. And in total sacrilege, during the last week of camp his fighters drink gallons of water and, via the manipulation of electrolytes, come the morning of weigh-ins they've pissed out at least seven pounds of water weight.

One afternoon I found Mike in the Zuffa corporate kitchen, and while grubbing a *Dolce Diet* recipe of wild salmon, sautéed string beans, and mashed sweet potatoes, I grilled him on his approach.

So, Mike, how has weight cutting evolved over the last twenty years?

"It hasn't. Turn of the century, and I mean the early 1900s, boxers would layer heavy clothes and plastics, stop eating, and sweat off the weight. They'd dehydrate and starve themselves for days, sometimes weeks, forcing their bodies to submit, but they paid a heavy price. And that was their health. That's the way a lot of guys still lose weight, and it's ridiculous. I'm on the other side of the scale—adhering to basic nutritional principles, I keep my guys healthy."

Joe Rogan has talked at length about fighters stepping on the scales at weigh-ins, and due to their sunken cheeks and eyes, he knows right then they're gonna lose.

"No question about it. In 2008, Daniel Cormier was captain of the U.S. Olympic wrestling team, and while losing weight [the old-fashioned way], his body completely shut down. They rushed him to the hospital, and the doctors, seeing how bad off he was, wouldn't let him compete. It's a shame, but adhering to those old-school principles crushed his Olympic dreams."

Explain, please.

"Well, I focus on the health of the athlete. That's number one. Using common-sense strategies based on whole foods, I keep my athletes as healthy as possible during the most unhealthy part of their training. This includes a diet based on nutrients that [have] sustained our species since the dawn of time. I get them off the pills, the powders, the potions, all the crazy fad diets and secret weight-loss tricks—I bring them back to the basics, and it works. I preach it and I hope to re-educate athletes, and ordinary people—this is what we truly need."

What do you do when a fighter slips?

"Each person is different. Regarding carrot and stick, I want nothing to do with the stick. My athletes slip, I treat them like adults. I find out why they slipped, what was the problem, what were the options at that time. Did they make an informed decision? Did they say, 'Yes, I'm consciously choosing to eat this now, though I know it's going to set my training back three days and balloon my bodyweight seven

Chris Weidman makes weight, *UFC 162*.

pounds.' I'm the coach, the trusted advisor—but you're an adult, the boss, captain of the ship. After the slip, there's no reason to dwell on it, we need to build back up and wipe out the consequences. I keep my responses very critical, very clean and professional. I always tell my athletes the exact truth. I tell them where they fucked up, when they fucked up, and why they fucked up—but I always help them find a way out of it. The important thing is to stop the slip. If Vitor calls me and says, 'Man, I got a sweet tooth and I'm craving something really bad, what should I have?' I'll ask what's available, what's in front of you, what's in your house, what's in your wife's purse, what's down the street? All my guys call me. After one or two fights, we develop a strong relationship."

Okay, so tell me about a slip.

"Okay. During Rampage's big weight loss, I stayed with him for eleven weeks before the fight. Everything was going good. Then, maybe six weeks into camp I'm in the kitchen around midnight and I hear a dog barking outside, really freaking out. I go to the door, and there's Rampage's assistant sneaking across the lawn, clutching a McDonald's bag. I stick my head out and ask what's going on. She jumps, hems and haws, then confesses that she's delivering Rampage food. So I walk down to his window, and on the ground there's an empty milkshake cup, a few crumpled bags. I confronted him, and he dropped his head and told me, 'I messed up, I messed up.'

"McDonald's in the middle of the night—that's a pretty big 'mess up' when you're preparing to fight Machida. I don't care who you are, at that level you need to be in the best shape of your life. Anyway, the fight ended in a split decision [Rampage won], but if he didn't slip those few times, who knows, [the decision] might've been unanimous."

So you're helping with the entire mental game?

"Diet is just a slice of fight camp. There's also the lifestyle, the rest, the recuperation, the support system—I help with all the influences, internal and external. Nutritional, emotional, financial stresses—they all impact a camp. If a fighter's going through shit with his girl, or wife, there's

nothing more detrimental. I also monitor the workouts, to eliminate overtraining and mental burnout."

But your books focus on diet . . .

"That's the foundation. If your diet isn't right, every cellular function in the body suffers. Skip breakfast and lunch, come two o'clock the average office worker feels like shit—they lose energy, cognitive ability, timing. Performance dulls and diminishes. Imagine the effect on a UFC fighter in full training camp. That's when the room for error is negligible. No, it's not negligible, it's zero. That's the irony; diet is such a dramatic part of the game, but most fans *and* most athletes don't see it. There's more drama filming a sweaty fighter punching heavy bags and running sprints—but watching him eat healthy meals, kind of boring."

BACKSTAGE

"Victorious warriors win first and then go to war, while defeated warriors go to war first and then seek to win."
—SUN TZU, *The Art of War*

Backstage during the pre-fight press conferences, or during the weigh-ins, at first look it's just a group of athletes milling about, shooting the shit. But wander close and you'll note the thousand-yard stares, the anxious fidgeting; closer still and you *feel* the low-octave hum. That nervous energy only intensifies as the fight draws near. Come fight night, back in the change rooms it's so thick that walking through with my camera, I step as quietly as possible and try to avoid any eye contact. For each fighter the pressure continues to ratchet until in the hallway he hears, "Let's roll, baby! Let's roll!"

That's the battle cry from UFC fight coordinator Burt Watson, a lifelong veteran of the fight game. This folksy bespectacled fellow, shuffling down the hallways, poking his head into change rooms, is the man tasked with ensuring the backstage happenings run smooth and on time. Fighters as a whole are a ragtag bunch—in the havoc there's always a missing mouthguard, or torn trunks, or a delayed flight—and with the heavy tension, these mishaps threaten a code red meltdown.

After managing Joe Frazier, Michael Spinks, and a slew of others, Burt knows more than anyone the pressures bearing down on a fighter. Maybe that empathy is rooted in his upbringing. Growing up in Buford, North Carolina, during the 1950s, at just five years old he'd enter the local grocery store, head downcast, and hand a note to the clerk. This was a different era, a parallel universe, it seems, when he describes how he'd stand silent as white customers brushed past, filling their baskets. Welcome to segregation, when your skin precluded you from touching the merchandise, or even looking at a white person. When you were "treated no better than a damn dog," Burt told me—then he recalled with pride the marches and demands for equal treatment, and the changes his generation spurred.

Then came The Fight of the Century: Muhammad Ali versus Joe Frazier, Madison Square Garden, 1971. At the time Burt was managing "Smoking" Joe, and leading up to the bout, after so much suffering via racism, and so much progress on civil rights, Muhammad Ali shouted to the world: "[Frazier is] the other type of Negro, he's not like me. There are two types of slaves. Frazier's worse than you to me. . . . One day he might be like me, but for now he works for the enemy."

For a black man in the early 1970s, this was the most demeaning bitch-slap. And it came from nowhere. During Ali's three-year expulsion from the fight world—broke and desperate, no means of feeding his family—it was Frazier who helped him with cash and public support. So why did Ali turn on his close friend? Because as a student of ancient warfare Ali knew it'd take more than left hooks and jabs to rattle his opponent. Come opening bell he wanted Frazier so angry, so confused, he'd bungle his fight strategy.

"Fights are won and lost backstage," Burt told me. "When [Michael] Spinks fought Tyson, I'll never forget, we're in the locker room and Spinks looks great. He's been training hard, got his head right, and an hour before the bell I'm looking around and I don't see him. I wander down to the bathroom, and there he is, sitting on the toilet, blank-staring at the wall . . . Ah shit, somehow during that hundred-foot walk from the dressing room to the stall, he'd lost it, beat himself, and there was nothing I could do to bring him back."

Roughly an hour before a fighter's call time, the cut-men head to the change rooms and sit the fighter in a chair. They unpack supplies while making small talk, and under constant watch of an Athletic Commission official they wrap the fighter's hands. It's an intense rite of passage signaling the end of a long camp, and it evokes countless metaphors, least of which is going to war with a medieval priest pronouncing his blessing.

"When you come to the arena and get your hands wrapped," Jon Fitch, a top welterweight contender recently released from the UFC, explained, "the fear escalates. There are literally times when you're warming up that you think, What am I doing here? I should just leave. I'm thirty-five years old, I have a college degree, what am I doing?"

"You get the bubble guts," said former lightweight UFC champion Frankie Edgar. "The anxiety is so intense, you wish you could speed it up and walk out right then."

I love photographing this scene because after the fists are gauzed and taped, there's no turning back. The tension is fucking awesome, and no camera—still or rolling—can capture the emotion in the room. "When they're getting taped, I go up and touch their pants," Burt told me, "you know, to make sure they're clean, and just the way a guy's breathing, I can tell if they're scared shitless."

Afterward, backstage and awaiting Burt's call, fighters pace, stretch a bit, watch live fights on the wall monitor. Every once in a while the video crew enters, the camera lights splash on, and the fighters posture for the live

Following page: José Aldo (top) and Antonio Rogério Nogueira having their hands taped.
Opposite: Chad Mendes—countdown.

audience—throw punches at the lens, offer a brief smile or a raised index finger. Then the crew departs, and it's back to the slow simmer.

At this point in the journey, a fighter must relax and control his nerves. The dreaded adrenaline dump—hands sweating, heart pumping, pupils dilated—is more dangerous than any competitor. To cope, some fighters shadowbox, some drill with coaches, some even run the halls.

Firas Zahabi, head trainer at Tristar Gym in Montreal, and some say the mastermind behind Georges St-Pierre, first works his fighter into a steady sweat, then he assesses the fighter's mental state. "If he's too calm, I might slap him a few times, try to rile him up. If he's too nervous, I'll talk him down. It also depends on his opponent: if the guy is more technical, or in better shape, I get my fighter fired up to charge—because anything can happen those first few minutes. It's only in the later rounds that technique comes into play. Or if it's the opposite situation, and my guy is more technical, I coach him to weather that first barrage."

THE WALKOUT

In the past few years I've shadowed countless fighters as they enter the arena—the team emerging from the tunnel, tracked by the live cameras, favorite song pumping, fans reaching for a touch of cloth, and that rising roar greeting: Anderson Silva, Jon Jones, Nick and Nate Diaz, Benson Henderson, Rory MacDonald, Georges St-Pierre, B.J. Penn, Tito Ortiz, Junior dos Santos, Cain Velasquez.

It's always a rush—but even more thrilling is a moment the entire arena shares: when the undercard fights end, the lights dim, murmurs sweep the darkness, and as the tension stretches *just so*, the trill of synthesizer melody cuts through and the velveteen sea erupts. Every time, no matter how

Jon Jones, in the garden.

many events you attend, no matter how exhausted or hungover you feel, your forearms pock and your gaze arcs skyward.

It's hard not to equate this ritual with some sort of modern religion. More Mao than Billy Graham, but still—the arena as cathedral; ten, fifteen thousand united in collective ecstasy beneath those *Blade Runner* monitors. Sure, Dana White is an avowed atheist, but even this song—most think it's "Teenage Wasteland," but the real title is "Baba O'Riley"—was penned by Pete Townshend in homage to his spiritual guru, Meher Baba.

These religious undercurrents infuse *the moment*, and I often imagine a peasant *right then* zapped from the Dark Ages to now—no comprehension of electricity, much less recorded music or pixels—but he knows fighting, and staring up at these giant humans battling in the sky, I'm sure he'd scream with the throng and make sense later.

CLIMBING THE STEPS

So we're in this cathedral, just steps from the cage, watching our fighter strip down to only gloves and trunks, naked but for the sacrifice of his preparation—those eight weeks of physical, mental, and, yes, *spiritual* toil. How fitting that ancient mystics regarded the octagon as a symbol of rebirth and resurrection, hence throughout Europe all those eight-sided baptismal fonts.

Our fighter hugs his teammates, and alone he raises his muscled arms in a cross, submitting to inspection from on high—and it's also worth noting this isn't solely a Judeo-Christian metaphor. The cross as symbol predates the crucifix. Predates even ancient Egypt's ankh. Archeologists have even discovered crosses painted on the walls of Stone Age caves.

"It's such a surreal moment," John Fitch said, "standing [on deck], you're getting sent off to war, and that's when you have to kill the fear. That's when I tell myself I've done everything I could during the eight weeks leading up to the

fight. If you haven't properly trained, the fear gets worse and overcomes you. But I'm pretty diligent [during camp], so I'm able to squash the fear during the walkout and grease-up period. And climbing the cage stairs, that's where I shake it off. When I walk into the cage, one of the first things I do is yell, to get my mindset in the right place. It's my war cry, announcing I'm ready to go, I'm here, let's do this."

THE FIGHT

The cage door closes. The bolt drops. The ref signals *Fight*, and it's on. Circling, weaving for efficient angles, or charging straight ahead—*now* is when a fighter tests his resolve. Can he implement that fight plan? Round after brutal round, ignore the creeping fatigue, the throbbing knee, blood stinging the eyes—or does he say to himself, *Fuck, he's too strong . . . I'm cramping . . . just survive this next round . . . no shame in a decision, if I clinch . . .*

Either way, moves and techniques had better occur via reflex because as this internal monologue reveals, *now* it's a battle of wills. The only unsettled question is who's *will* is gonna break first?

MMA is a beautiful sport, if not always on the physical plane—where the long clinches and circling sometimes prove tedious—then on that higher, more ethereal plane. The plane of the spirit. Where each feint, tie-up, and kick is unleashed not merely to damage, but to chip away at an opponent's will.

Only after visiting gyms, training with fighters, overhearing their intimate conversations, did I appreciate how a bout equals more than the sum of its violence. Forget the surface. What you're watching is a battle of character, resolve, courage in the face of pain, and doggedness in the face of exhaustion.

The Walkout, with Daron Cruickshank.

"This is the first thing I am thinking about," Lyoto Machida explained. "I am not the biggest, the brightest, or the best, but it is all about breaking the spirit of whoever is in front of me . . . I sense weakness, and I focus on that. You sense which weapons you have to take away from him."

But can you actually feel when an opponent breaks?

"Yes, I feel a collapse, and I know at any moment the fight will be over."

Nearly every fighter embraced this philosophy: Break the will, break the will. Vitor Belfort, however, cautioned, "You must be careful. If you are trying to break [an opponent's will], and you don't, then what happens? You break your own will. I learned that early. Get empty, that's the secret to success. Empty the mind, become water. You cannot stop water—water finds a way, just let it go."

During our conversation I was surprised to hear Vitor, like Lyoto, apply his combat philosophies to everyday life. Like spilling sand from one palm to the other: life as art, art as life. Vitor told me: "If I am going into negotiation and I want this direction, what happens if I don't [achieve it]? So go there freely—have your strategy, but remain flexible. Survive the storm, the thunders and hurricanes inside the fight, and enjoy your time. We have max twenty-five minutes, so enjoy it. Make it the best twenty-five minutes of your life, that way you don't have any regrets. I have so many regrets in my life—things I should have done, and I didn't—so that's why I tell people, 'Everything you want to do, do it now, not tomorrow. Don't wait for the next round, this may be the last.'"

During *UFC 152* in Toronto in September 2012, Vitor caught champion Jon Jones in a vicious armbar. Lifting his

hips, hyperextending the elbow, and straining for a submission, Vitor heard a *pop!* and thinking the joint broke, he released—allowing Jones to wiggle free. The entire arena stood screaming, few expecting such an underdog feat.

Vitor tried again and again to repeat the maneuver, to the disbelief of many, dropping to the canvas and pulling guard—which opened him to Jones's patented ground-and-pound elbow attack. Early in the fourth round, Jones transitioned from those elbows to an americana submission, and forced Vitor to tap out, thus ending the Brazilian's dreams of recapturing the UFC light heavyweight belt.

So I had to ask—this strategy, was that *water*?

Vitor gazed at the ground, gently shaking his head. "No, I had him, I did—but I kept trying to force it. This is something you must overcome in a fight, because though [the armbar] worked once, I should not have kept trying it over and over. I pulled guard the next time, he elbowed me, and the fight changed. It was back and forth—I went to his field, now he's in my field. I'm punching him, controlling, then I pulled guard again . . . I made so many mistakes in that fight. Mistakes I regret, big-time. I haven't watched the fight because I am still so sad. People say, 'You did great'—but I didn't. I should have won the fight. That fight I should have won everywhere. On the ground, even standing up I was winning, I was beating him and then I pull guard because I was so [fixated] on doing something that worked early. I kept trying to find his arm. So, no, that was *not* water—I should have flowed, but I didn't, and it cost me."

It's fascinating how any missteps along this journey—ineffective training, poor fight strategy, improper diet, backstage nerves—weaken a fighter and even if he lies to others and tells the world he's never felt better, during the fight this doubt eats at him.

Which brings us to perhaps the most important decision a fighter makes: *In which camp should I train?*

Or, couched in terms of the hero's journey: *Which grizzled old-timer shall I choose as my mentor?*

5: FIGHT CLUB

"MMA is not a fucking team sport."
—UFC PRESIDENT DANA WHITE

TECHNICALLY, D.W.'S RIGHT—each fighter must scale those steel steps and cross that Octagon threshold alone. But pause and rewind the tape, and watch him backpedaling onto the deck, submitting to inspection, then hugging his trainer—but wait, *there!*—just as he closes his eyes during that final embrace, from *that* point he's on his own . . . *right?*

Not really. Sure, during the bout he's the one enduring kicks and elbows, but his team sits cageside, shouting instructions, and between rounds they're placating his doubts and laying down next-round strategy.

So let's keep reversing the footage: he and his team back-step through the crowd and into the tunnel's holding area, where together they pace under camera lights . . . in the locker room he warms up with his team . . . the team arrives at the arena . . . the team flies to the host city . . . back in the gym, all day, every day, the team is together.

You get the point. A fighter is rarely alone. He lives and trains with a camp.

But not all camps are created equal. Each boasts its own philosophies, hierarchy, social mores, geographic pros and cons—which is why "Which camp should I choose?" is one of the most important forks on the journey.

THE COMMUNE: TEAM ALPHA MALE

After parking in a strip-mall complex on the outskirts of Sacramento, California, I gaze through the bugged-up windshield and spot a sign for Ultimate Fitness. I grab my workout bag and head inside, ducking from the summer heat into the cool, familiar clinking of weights, thuds on heavy bags, the whiff of lemony disinfectant and sweat.

Top: Team Alpha Male.
Bottom: Urijah Faber, adrenaline junkie.

It's a typical MMA gym—boxing ring, mats—until turning toward the register, there's a massive cutout of Urijah Faber, arm raised triumphant.

Most members of Team Alpha Male wrestled in college; and that wrestling culture carries over. "You grow up competing against your friends," Urijah said, "going through this crazy regimen together, and that brings you close. In the wrestling world, your first major competition is to decide the best guy in the room for the varsity spot."

Joseph Benavidez fought for the inaugural UFC flyweight championship during *UFC 152* in September 2012 in Toronto. I sat with him and Urijah, and we discussed the team's structure, ethos, etc.: "It's a unique approach, as we don't have a head coach," Benavidez told me. "We all help, and we all want what's best for the others. It's like combining our wills into one; and what I mean is, if it's just me wanting a win, that's nothing compared to Urijah, Chad, T.J., all of us wanting that win, and all of us putting in the work to make it happen. That's why we're a real team, and not just a camp."

So how do you choose?

Joe: "You need to find people who bring out the best in you, other like-minded people. I don't want to hang with some dude I've got nothing in common with, where we don't get along. Being from New Mexico, the easy thing would've been to train with [renowned MMA coach and New Mexico resident] Greg Jackson. But now I'm with family, and at Jackson's camp, where 100 fighters are flocking in and out every day, I'd just get lost in the shuffle."

If you don't have a leader, who sets the schedule?

Urijah: "Well, every fighter has specific needs, and that's why we have so many different coaches. It's like coming into a restaurant and looking over the menu. 'I'll take a bit of this wrestling, some of that jiu-jitsu—some muay Thai, American kickboxing, boxing.' A fighter customizes the meal based on his weaknesses, or needs."

Joe: "It's a very open environment; no one gets upset

when I go outside [the camp] and seek other coaches, stay with them for a week, bring them in. Now that I'm actually making a living from the sport, I can afford to bring outside coaches in for weeks at a time—not only for me, but the team also benefits in seeing what else is out there. A fighter has to explore all options. MMA is still so new that no one has a lock on all the techniques and training methods. Even if you're at the top of the game, you're still learning. There's just so many aspects to the sport."

That's great for general training, but who determines fight strategy?

Urijah: "If someone's got [an upcoming] bout, the team watches tape on the opponent and writes down what they think. Then different guys work together, some step up and help coach. Justin Buchholz helps map fight plans for many of us."

Joe: "'You are your best coach,'—I love that saying. You know what you need, what your body needs, and you know what you should do in the ring."

Urijah: "We don't need somebody to tell us, 'Okay, this is what you *must* do in this next fight.' Sure, there are general themes, weaknesses we look for, but it's up to [each fighter] to step in there and compete."

MMA training is difficult, so what if I wanna sleep in and skip morning practice?

Joe: "The team holds you accountable. There's always someone that says, 'Hey, come in at this time . . . and, 'Where were you this morning? I needed you.' Every day they push you. Like when you go against a teammate who got the best of you—you want to get him back. So it's good to know you're always gonna be challenged by your team."

Urijah. "We train 24/7 because this is our job—what the fuck else are you gonna do, sit around and watch TV? Most people think our sport is difficult and unappealing, and probably pretty scary. But for us, if you're training three to six hours a day, preparing non-stop, it's like riding a bike—you're not scared to ride a bike once you learn. The first time you start pedaling on your own, of course that's scary. But for us, after hours and hours of wrestling, sparring, and hitting mitts—all that preparation nullifies the fear. You become immune to it. It's funny to look across the other side and realize how crazy we are. Like, we fucking fight our closest friends *all day*. We beat each other senseless. Joseph [Benavidez] has ten stitches in his lip right now because T.J. [Dillashaw] tried to kick him in the face and instead caught him with a knee. But it's no big deal. Together we shed blood, sweat, and tears. We're the tightest knit group because we share those things."

So I gel with the guys, I'm a wrestler, how do I join Team Alpha Male?

Urijah: "Just sign up at the gym. Everyone's welcome. But from there it's sink or swim. We beat the fuck out of each other. There is no pussyfooting around—the weakest get weeded out quick, and what's left is a fucking core group of bad asses, and that core sets the tone. It's really like, Show up and if you earn a spot on the team, then you're part of the team. If you're holding people back, then we'll ask you to leave [the pro classes]. You can come back after you've taken some of the general classes. Either way, I never try to talk a fighter into coming out here because it never works. Once you talk someone into coming out, it's your fault if it doesn't work. This is a self-motivated sport. If you're getting pushed [into MMA], then you're in the wrong fucking sport. This shit's hard."

So is it a team sport?

Joe: "Listen, I consider them brothers and they've all helped me get to this point, and I feel as though I've helped them. So—"

Urijah: "We don't compete at the same time, so it's not really a team sport. But it is a family sport."

Top: Urijah Faber, training with Dustin Akbari.
Bottom: Joseph Benavidez on the treadmill.

THE MASTER: ANDERSON SILVA

Anderson "The Spider" Silva is the greatest martial artist to ever walk the earth. That's a bold claim, I know, and it sends the mind reeling, envisioning some mythical Shaolin monk wandering the Asian countryside, brutalizing foes far from royal courtyards, historians, or cameras.

Ever?

Yes, ever.

"Martial arts have advanced more in the last ten years than in the last ten thousand," Dana White often quips—and he's right. In the seventeenth century, our mythical Shaolin monk might have mastered rudimentary kung fu, but it's doubtful he had an inkling of European grappling, jiu-jitsu, or muay Thai.

Yet Anderson Silva reigns supreme in an age when every technique is just a *click* away. It's all there, for free, just search YouTube to learn the nuances of any kick, any punch, any submission. No small coincidence this martial arts advancement mirrors the growth of the virtual hive-mind.

A dedicated student of every combat discipline, The Spider holds black belts in muay Thai, judo, tae kwon do, and jiu-jitsu. He trains wrestling, boxing—hell, the guy's even grappled with an indigenous Brazilian tribe. Yeah, he's suffered four losses during his fifteen years competing in MMA, but again, this ain't boxing, where trainers and promoters duck tough fights in order to pad records and rake cash—in the Octagon, fighters face all worthy challengers.

That said, the man hasn't lost in seven years. Hardly the most brutal or the fastest striker, Anderson brings into the cage a grace and poise rarely seen in competitive fighting. It's more ballet than combat, and what I mean is, *real* ballet—where those years of blisters, muscle strains, diet, hysterical tears—yield for us, the audience, a few minutes of onstage beauty that leaves us awed and cheering for more.

So he's the greatest. But having spent hours backstage with Anderson—prior to his bouts, prior to other fighters' bouts, even at other organizations' bouts—I grew most intrigued with his commitment to mentoring younger fighters. I've seen him coach, warm up, even wrap the hands of fighters that train not just at his gym but within his martial arts lineage.

Lineage. The term is seldom heard in American sports, and it's the great divide between wrestling and jiu-jitsu. Yeah, "Where'd you wrestle?" is a common question, but it's more an ice-breaker than anything else. Yet in Brazilian culture, "Who you train under?" seeks information regarding style, social mores, disposition, loyalties, even character. But Silva is different. Silva has transcended that query. Trite as it sounds: no longer is he the student, now he is the master.

Unlike most camps, Silva runs the show. Assembling trainers and sparring partners to help him prepare for a fight. Running drills. Giving feedback. This includes Steven Seagal, who claimed credit for the KO front kick that Silva unleashed on Vitor Belfort during *UFC 126* in February 2011. "People laugh," said Ed Soares, Silva's manager, "but I personally watched Seagal drill that kick with Silva at least two hundred times. No, he didn't teach him the kick, but he definitely helped refine it. Let's face it, at this point in Anderson's career, there's not much he doesn't know."

And like any great master, Silva not only fights but also spends time nurturing his own lineage. "In martial arts, it's important to give back," he told me, "to help those younger, just as I was helped. That's the way to make this world a better place. To give, not just take."

Top: Professor Silva.
Bottom: Silva warming up Paulo Bananada before his fight.

THE PHYSICIST: GREG JACKSON

That shimmering on the horizon, it's the future, and though we'll never reach it, you can bet your ass it's gonna up the game of nearly every endeavor. In MMA, there's no way to talk camps, strategy, or evolution without touching on trainer Greg Jackson.

By far, one of the most fascinating articles ever written on MMA appeared not in an industry publication but in *Popular Science* magazine.

In summary, "Cage Match: How Science Is Transforming the Sport of MMA Fighting" described how every MMA camp studies an opponent's prior fights and in turn formulates fight strategy to secure a win. This technique is as old as the antique film projector in your great-grandfather's attic. But with the rise of technology, not only are fights filmed and archived; now, in real-time, the FightMetric crew logs every punch, kick, takedown, knockdown, and submission attempt. At fights the data is displayed on a monitor near Joe Rogan, so he can call the live action while Mike Goldberg intersperses relevant stats.

Self-dubbed "the world's only comprehensive mixed martial arts statistics and analysis system," FightMetric provides stats for MMA. I've sat with the team backstage—each tech geek hunched inches from their screen, tapping away at game controllers as their assigned fighter throws and ducks.

Later, UFC producers comb these stats for trends—as does Greg Jackson. And that quantitative approach is what separates the legendary trainer from his peers. Like the baseball scouts portrayed in the movie *Moneyball*, Jackson spurns hunches and theories for empirical data. Tell him an inside leg kick is the best setup for an overhand right, and he'll say, *Show me*—and what that means is pull up the spreadsheet and prove it.

Previous page: Anderson Silva walking out with Paulo Bananada.

Jackson, however, quantum-leaps mere data crunching—

In 1928, mathematician John von Neumann proved to the world his "mini-max theorem, " which states that for every finite, zero-sum two-person game (e.g., an MMA fight), there exists a set of optimal choices; and a player can determine these choices via a decision tree or matrix. This framework for analyzing games in which two opponents make decisions to best each other is also called "game theory" or, simply, "Which move should I make next?"

Typical application involves a tic-tac-toe chart with each quadrant containing outcomes produced by the available choices. Appropriately enough, let's consider a game of tic-tac-toe: two players, nine squares = eighty-one quadrants representing every outcome. The math entails a bit of calculus, but it's so useful that psychologists, economists, global warming scientists, and now even MMA trainers use game theory to map the most efficient means of traveling from A to D.

In a fight, that means charting a path from touching gloves to KO while incurring the least damage. Jackson actually uses a subset of game theory known as extensive form game. Instead of simplistic charts, he maps out complex decision trees so he can answer questions like: "If Jon Jones throws an inside leg kick, what are the moves he can follow with? And which of those moves inflicts the most damage?"

"It's an exciting time to be a martial artist," Greg told me. "We are pushing the edges of fight theory. We have access to data and tools we've never had access to before: game theory, fractals. It's all new. [The theory of] relativity is just one hundred years old. So with combat and fight strategy, smarter men than me have tackled these problems, for thousands of years, but the world is now a smaller place. Everyone says Greece represented the highest form of evolution, but they didn't have access to systems from Mongolia or Thailand. Today, I can learn anything very quickly: from the Internet, videos, even jump on a plane. So of course our theory should eclipse anything before."

In regards to game theory, how do you map out a fight?

"First off, there is nothing tic-tac-toe about a dynamic system, it has to remain open-ended. It can't be planned. It's like chess. Think of a decision tree—you aren't trying to get from node-*x* to victory, you are trying to get to the node *before* victory. That allows options for failure. So you move along the decision tree to the best position."

As in moving toward side control (e.g., jiu-jitsu), where you can drop elbows, attempt an armbar or a Kimura, or move to full mount?

"Exactly. These optimum positions contain the most options, or clusters. It's like in chess, how you cluster pieces to shut off your opponent's choices. It's the same thing. Get yourself to the node with the most clusters, which still allows you to fail and return safely to the position and try something else."

When do you formulate strategy for a specific fight?

"When you're starting camp, you have to ID the parameters—how do you get to your opponent's safety zone, how do you mentally break them—because at the end of the day, if they are still conscious, you've got to break them. If they pass out before that happens, that's fine, but you don't control that. You only control putting yourself in the positions."

So there's a nexus between empirical analysis and breaking the spirit?

"Think about it. If you hit your opponent in the face, he may go unconscious, he may not—you can't control that, so you need to look at game theory in light of doing that over and over again—working toward and from a clustered node until the person quits or goes unconscious. That's why it is so important to fight for clusters, as opposed to specific moves. Forget the armbar—the

Greg Jackson (right) coaching.

armbar is just a single option off the node. The cluster is the important thing."

So tonight [UFC 159 on April 27, 2013, Jones versus Sonnen], *when Jon went right into Chael's strength, wrestling, was that part of breaking the will?*

"When GSP fought Koscheck the first time, people mapped how the fight was going to play out—but they never accounted for GSP attacking Koscheck's strength. Attacking an opponent's strength accelerates the breaking process. Sun Tzu wasn't always right when he said avoid your enemy's strengths and attack the weaknesses. He also said know yourself, and know your enemy; *and if you can outdo him where he is the strongest*, that's when you break him mentally."

Tangled up: John Cofer and Lance Palmer.

OR UNIVERSE RYU /RYU.COM

6: DO THE EVOLUTION

"It is not the strongest of the species that survives, nor the most intelligent, but the one most responsive to change."

—CHARLES DARWIN

EVOLUTION. Forget the unfounded religious arguments, it's proven: in the face of adversity, cells adapt, animals adapt, systems adapt. Evolve, or wither and perish.

弱肉強食: *The weak are meat the strong eat.*

Nowhere is this Japanese proverb truer than in MMA. No disrespect to Royce Gracie, but teleport that in-prime teen from the inaugural Octagon to now, and facing *any* modern UFC fighter, it's doubtful he'd survive two minutes. This isn't a put-down but praise to the seed he sowed. The seed that sprouted and survived harsh winds and drought, adapting, evolving, so now, two decades later, if that young Royce walked into a modern MMA gym and learned evolved skills from each style, if he trained daily with elite fighters and honed strategy with a revered coach—now that's an interesting hypothesis. If only we could compare two in-prime MMA fighters from different eras, two fighters shaped by wholly disparate techniques and philosophies. Scientists scour nature for such matched subjects, and instead must mock up experiments in the lab.

In 1969, to answer the question, *Who's the greatest heavyweight boxing champion of all time?* Murry Woroner, an advertising exec, commissioned a vacuum tube computer to calculate, round by round, the likely results of a Rocky Marciano versus Muhammad Ali bout. He then smuggled both fighters into a blacked-out Miami gym, and donning gloves and trunks, they re-enacted the computer simulation for the cameras.

In the end, the outcome of the famed Super Fight was based not on crunched data but Marciano's massive ego. After a feigned bloody back-and-forth battle, in the thirteenth round Marciano knocked Ali out. Later, on *The Dick Cavett Show*, Ali lambasted the simulation: "I'm gonna say right here on nationwide TV, looking right into the cameras, anybody who's connected with the computer . . . I thought it was really serious . . . but it's really a phony, it's not real . . . there's no such thing as a computer that can take Joe Louis's record and Jack Dempsey's . . . and [forecast] what would've happened the night they fought."

There it is. So we resign ourselves to barroom arguments, playing out these matchups over pitchers of beer. *Yah, so what if Joe Louis fought Mike Tyson? Or Sugar Ray Robinson fought Roy Jones Jr.? No, no, say Floyd Mayweather fought Sugar Ray Leonard . . .*

But in December 2012, in Seattle, Washington, UFC matchmakers delivered just such a bout. The *UFC on Fox 5* card featured not only Benson Henderson and Nate Diaz for the lightweight championship but also, to test our multi-era theory, B.J. Penn versus Rory MacDonald.

On one side of the cage was B.J. Penn, the jiu-jitsu giant-killer from MMA's golden era, squaring off against Rory MacDonald, the torchbearer for the new pure breed of MMA. Two prodigious fighters, each armed with the training, strategies, and mindset of their respective generations.

That's right—not only did these fighters emerge from different eras, they are both prodigies. In his book *Outliers,* Malcolm Gladwell argued that for the very best in any field, whether hockey, computer programming, or rock music, to reach the highest pinnacle of mastery, they *must* hone those skills over ten thousand hours. In support he offered real-world examples of Wayne Gretzky, Bill Gates, and The Beatles. Forget natural talent, he argues, genius springs from time at the grind. It's an appealing *and* appalling theory, depending on your work ethic, and both B.J. and Rory, from a young age, committed their lives to combat.

The GOAT: B.J. Penn with his World Jiu-Jitsu medal and Welterweight UFC belt.

B.J. PENN

The Prodigy. Homegrown in Hilo, Hawaii, B.J. Penn shocked the jiu-jitsu world in 2000 when, as the first non-Brazilian, he stormed through the black-belt division of the Jiu-Jitsu World Championships and captured the gold. There is no way to overstate this feat. After training seriously for just three years he earned his black belt faster than anyone on record . . . and now this.

"I was good right off the bat, nobody could pass my guard," B.J. told me. "I was so flexible, I didn't know what I was doing, but no one could ever pass my legs."

Despite how remarkable this sounds, don't think for a moment B.J. just wandered into the dojo and mastered the sport. He put in his ten thousand hours, on and off the mat. "There was a time jiu-jitsu haunted me," he said, "from seventeen to twenty-two [years old] it would never leave my head. I just could not get it out of my mind. Lying in bed, in the shower, or even fucking my girlfriend, I practiced moves day and night."

Spend enough time with enough elite UFC fighters and you realize they all share this trait—it might well be the virus that mutates *all* outliers, as there's just no other way to accumulate so many hours in such a short span.

"I remember flying to California," B.J. said, "I was only seventeen, and I don't know why, but I told this lady sitting next to me, I said, 'I think I found what I'm going to do for the rest of my life.'"

B.J. sacrificed everything for this obsession, abandoning the lush jungles of Hilo for the asphalt and grit of Northern California. There, he studied under Ralph Gracie, grandson of Carlos Gracie. Alone. A sheltered teen on foreign soil, he retreated into the dojo, drilling from dawn till dusk, entering tournaments on weekends. And every month or so, to vary his training, he traveled to Las Vegas and worked with John Lewis, a late-1990s MMA fighter and respected black belt.

Just so happened that John was also teaching Dana White and Lorenzo Fertitta jiu-jitsu. B.J. attended a private lesson in what is now the Zuffa headquarters' private gym. "John brought me to meet Dana and Lorenzo, and before we rolled, John whispered to me, 'Hey, don't go too hard on me today, I don't want these clients to think I'm no good.' After the session John mentioned that I might fight MMA, and Dana asked about my boxing. I told him I'd worry about boxing after I got my black belt. He told me, 'No, you should work on your hands now because striking doesn't come easy'—but I was thinking, I already got hands, buddy."

Jump forward a few years, and B.J. is in Brazil, hunched over a meal, hours before his final match of the Jiu-jitsu World Championships. "At lunch, I remember saying to myself, 'I'll never be in this situation again. If he gets me in an arm lock or foot lock, I just gotta let it break because I gotta win this match . . .'"

Now jump twelve years to the night before the *Fox 5* bout: B.J.'s lying on the hotel floor, stretching out and reminiscing. "I will never forget that day," he says, smiling at the ceiling.

Like many turn-of-the-millennium MMA fighters, B.J. followed a winding path into the cage: as a kid he obsessed on professional wrestling, practicing the backyard techniques in the grass with his brothers, jumping from trees. "I was always into WWF–type stuff, so we'd do a thing we called 'moves.' One guy does a suplex, another body slams, and we'd just keep doing that over and over. That's how I learned to read—in bed each night I'd flip through WWF magazines, trying to learn as much as I could. I was into martial arts, and that was the next stage for me."

At fourteen he started boxing. "My first combat sport was boxing, but you couldn't really call it boxing because it was just kids from my high school fighting each other. Once in a while I'd stop by the rec center and spar with

Top: B.J. Penn, the first non-Brazilian to storm through the black-belt division of the Jiu-Jitsu World Championships and earn gold, watches his finals win.
Bottom: B.J. trains with Makua Rothman.

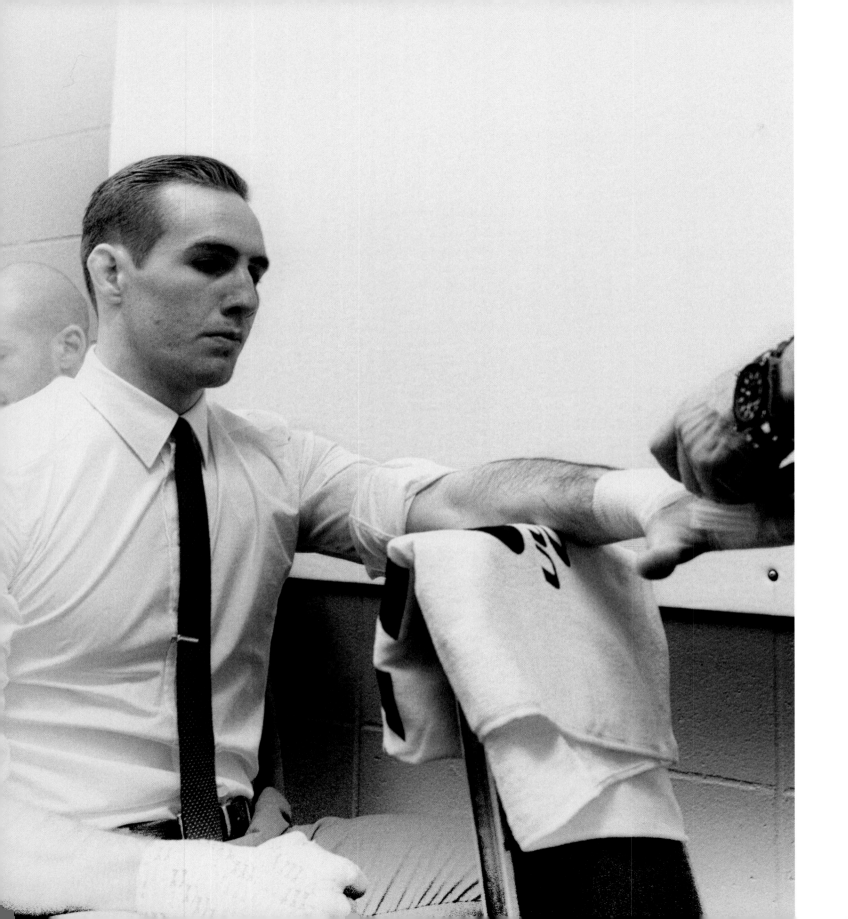

different guys, but I never took formal training because I thought I could do it myself, I was hard-headed."

After winning the Worlds, B.J. returned to California and started wrestling at West Valley Junior College. He also trained at the American Kickboxing Academy, in San Jose, California, under the tutelage of famed kickboxer Javier Mendez. His transition from jiu-jitsu to MMA, in hindsight, seems fated because just a few months following his world jiu-jitsu win, Dana and Lorenzo purchased the UFC.

That's right, the same guys he'd rolled with a few years earlier. And for their second event, *UFC 31* in May 2001, they called on him to fight Joey Gilbert. And B.J. TKO'd him in the first round. Seven months later he fought Jens Pulver for the UFC lightweight championship. B.J. lost a majority decision, but after several succeeding wins he fought again for the lightweight belt—this time to a draw against Caol Uno. Frustrated, he jumped at the next title shot, moving up a weight class to battle Matt Hughes. Against all odds, B.J. proved true the old-school jiu-jitsu maxim: *Great technique bests size and strength any day of the week.*

Now back to our Era versus Era theorem. Or rather, "If we pit two in-prime prodigious MMA fighters, each using the training and fight strategies from their respective eras, who will triumph?"

Of course, B.J. as a test subject doesn't seem germane, as he, after all, trained inside the ever-evolving AKA gym, home to countless veterans, rising stars, and enlightened trainers. Environment shapes, Darwin might say. But in 2002, B.J. packed his bags and returned to Hawaii, where he would remain for much of his career. Back in those lush jungles he gathered local coaches and fighters into a self-made camp, replicating the early days of MMA, before elite teams littered the stateside maps. A moth preserved in amber, physically and mentally intact but adaptively stalled.

Canadian Psycho: Rory MacDonald.
Previous pages: B.J. Penn with pro surfer/skater Kalani David in P.M. Tenore's [RVCA founder and president] office; B.J. weighs in; B.J. and crew backstage.

Not to say he wasn't nurtured. Or maybe that was the problem. "In Hawaii there are no professional sports," B.J. told me. "The fighters are the professional sports, that's why fighting is so big. That's who they look to, and who I represent. My people get behind me, and I don't want to let them down."

But it's my contention that this Jurassic Park environment shielded him from the evolutionary pressures of the modern MMA world. Sure, prior to each fight he flew in sparring partners, and for some fights he trained on the mainland at the private RVCA gym, in Costa Mesa, California—but that's hardly a substitute for the day-in, day-out stresses that mold most fighters. And as for fight strategy, in his memoir, *Why I Fight: The Belt Is Just an Accessory*, B.J. trumpets his slogan: Just Scrap.

Forget game theory, and forget decision trees—B.J. enters the cage to brawl.

RORY MACDONALD

There's no debate, Rory MacDonald represents the new breed. Wanna talk lab experiments? Plop any MMA devotee in a sterile room of beakers and blue flames, and no question in a glass bowl he'd sprinkle the following genes: *six-foot frame, mesomorphic physique, stone-cold demeanor, anti-social tendencies, kinesthetic aptitude, above-average intelligence . . .*

Oh, and don't forget that outlier-like obsession.

After Rory's only loss, a last-second heartbreaker to Carlos Condit, he abandoned his hometown of Kelowna, British Columbia, for the big city and elite coaching of Tristar Gym in Montreal, Quebec.

In so many ways Rory personifies the ten-thousand-hours theory. "I wasn't naturally talented," he told me. "I first walked into the gym like a fool. Maybe I had some scrappiness, and maybe I was mentally tough, but I sucked at fighting. I just wasn't any good."

Yet, head bowed and humbled he stuck with it, worked and worked, never mind the clumsy pubescent body he forced to kick bags, shoot doubles, lift weights—hell or high water he would mold and master the damn thing, in the process racking up hours as if in a video game: *1,000, 2,000, 3,000,...* "I was always dedicated to my craft. I love martial arts. To get good fast you have to love what you're doing. If you don't have a passion for something, you'll never excel at it."

After administrators booted him from school for truancy and other juvenile mayhem, he dove headlong into training—seven days a week, hanging round the club until nightfall. "I left with the last guy. I'm more passionate than most, and that's probably why I got good so fast."

That and the sophisticated approach of Tristar. "My training is very intense and programmed," Rory said. "The moment I step in the gym I know my plan, I know exactly what I'm working on."

THE FIGHT: *UFC ON FOX 5*

After the walkouts B.J. and Rory stand under their respective banners. Bruce Buffer bellows into the mic, and, elbows crossed on the Octagon walkway, I glance left to right and it's clear our theory is strained. These are hardly equal specimens: Rory stands six-foot and monstrous, dwarfing the five-nine B.J.

They're both welterweights, what gives? Damn it. I flashback to our primer on weight loss: over an eight-week camp a two-hundred-pound fighter will shed ten, twenty pounds, denying desserts, and training three times a day, and the last week he cuts salt and sweats and pisses out the rest.

That's how 99.9 percent of current fighters roll, including Rory.

Not B.J.

The Hawaiian jiu-jitsu master holds to that old-school maxim: *Great technique bests size and strength any day of the week* . . .

Sounds good to me. I'm all about Helio Gracie. But glancing across the Octagon, at Rory, all titan-like, then at B.J., I remember how the much smaller Helio had his arm snapped by Masahiko Kimura during their fabled match.

The ref starts the action, and it's an old-school battle for sure. Rory kicks B.J. in the chest. Manhandles him against the cage. Throws a left elbow that nearly drops him. Forget the size/reach advantage, Rory is too fast, too conditioned, too technical to catch or counter. A tiger mauling its prey for five minutes.

Between rounds B.J. slumps on his stool, and a guy from his corner yells, "Use your face, use your fucking face!"

I have no idea what this means . . .

The second round starts and it's more of the same: Rory throws stiff jabs and level-10 kicks, short elbows to the face. Joe Rogan laments B.J.'s lack of strategy, and he lays blame on the corner: "Unfortunately they didn't have much to say to him technically, it was mostly just cheerleading." Then, after another textbook blitz: "Oh, brilliant combination—left hook, right hand by Rory, then a front kick to cap it off."

Rory drives a vicious kick to the liver and B.J. doubles over, holding his side, cringing. Hurts to watch, and sucks even more to recount, because like most MMA fans I revere B.J. and his accomplishments, and I'm angry that this old-era code has blinded him to that even wiser truth: 弱肉強食; *The weak are meat the strong eat.*

Ever the warrior, B.J. survives the three rounds, but via unanimous decision he drops his fourth loss in six fights. No, this wasn't the equally matched experiment we'd hoped for, but on the flip side, the results bolster this new-era approach.

Evolution triumphs.

Again.

Rory MacDonald and B.J. Penn in the cage.
Following pages: Rory warms up backstage with Firas Zahabi; Rory MacDonald, way of the Bushidō 武士道.

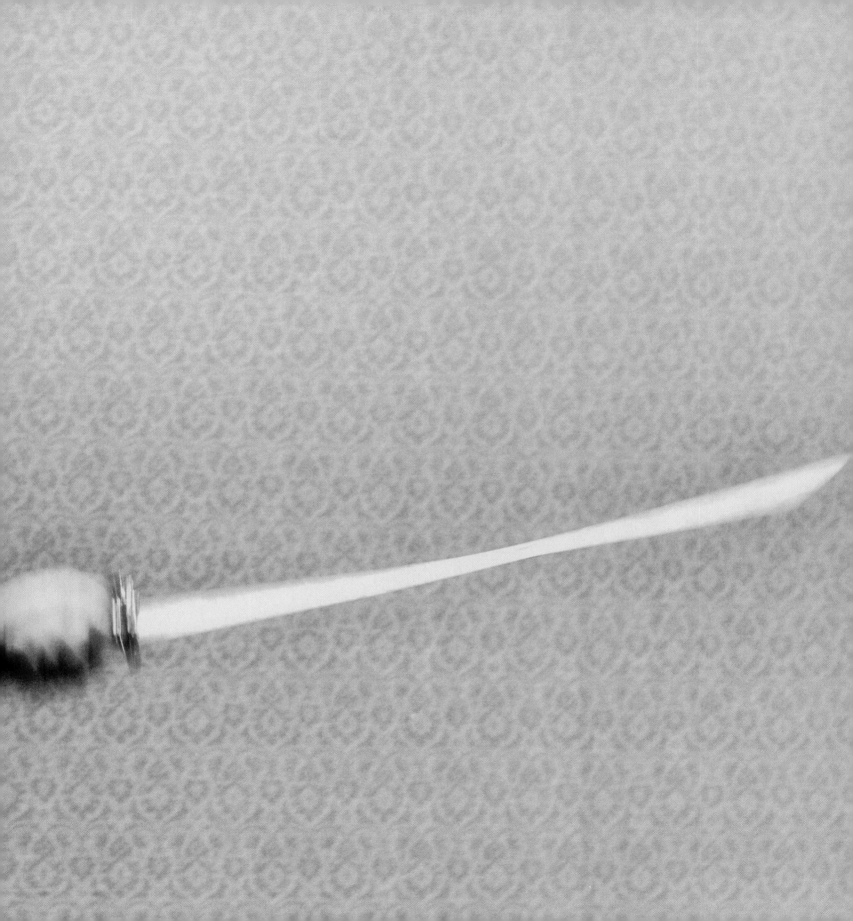

7: THE MOUNTAIN

THE MOUNTAIN. It's such an apt metaphor for any sport: those hundreds of thousands scaling the rocky slopes, risking anything to reach the next crag, trying to remain focused, inspired, *don't look down*, delusional even—whatever it takes to climb higher and stay fixed on the peak—the peak where the champion stands surveying his kingdom to the horizon.

It's gonna be so awesome up there, that view, and everyone knowing I'm the best in the world. I'll sacrifice anything, I don't care. . .

But when you consider the long odds, clearly it's the path, not the pinnacle that defines the journey. And even if the goal is achieved, take note: most champions hold the belt on average just 1.55 fights. That's right. Scan through UFC history and you'll find 55 champions, who (as of this writing) on-the-whole successfully defended their titles a mere eighty-five times (stats courtesy of UFC editorial director Thomas Gerbasi). Now that's daunting math.

So to understand the sport we must turn from the summit and assess the lifetime of dedication and work, the struggles to conquer the fear of falling, and the fear of injury, the will to wipe away the tears and continue climbing, all while knowing at any moment the rock in your grip might crumble.

After years of training in a single combat discipline, an athlete transitions to MMA, enters an amateur event, wins, enters a few more, compiles a winning record, joins a respected team. Fights a professional MMA bout or two, then auditions for *The Ultimate Fighter* (*TUF*), the UFC's reality TV series that's designed to function as the company's minor league.

That's where I first met Myles Jury. He entered season 15 riding a nine-fight win streak, all stoppages during the first round, and because he suffered a knee injury during *TUF* season 13, and was forced to leave the show without

Rashad Evans lost in thought.

a bout, people knew his name. And these people, including his *TUF* coach, Dominick Cruz, expected big things. In his first *TUF* fight, the Vegas bookies picked him to rout Al Iaquinta. The fighters entered the cage, split two hard-fought rounds, fought a tiebreaker, and Iaquinta emerged the winner.

After the show I found Myles backstage. He was unhappy about the split decision, so I switched the subject and we talked San Diego, jiu-jitsu, and Swami's, a surf break in Encinitas, California. Rough life, I told him, hanging on the beach, training all morning, lunch then nap, train again, grab dinner and a movie. He laughed. We agreed to hook up for a surf—but forget Swami's, that over-crowded long-board zoo, I told him, come up to Newport and test your skills.

I never thought he'd call. But he did, and after a night session we grabbed fish tacos and beers and shot the shit.

"I love training, love to fight, but getting in the water, just paddling out, there's nothing better. Anything to keep from burning out."

Burning out? You're just starting this climb—

"In the UFC, yes, but I've already been fighting ten years. And with wrestling and tae kwon do, it's not like I just walked into the gym."

Okay, so where do you see yourself in the next ten years?

"I think about that all the time. I know I can't fight forever, and I don't want to be fifty years old, working at somebody else's gym. So I'm trying to be smart with the decisions I make. Not just with fighting, but also my investments. It's such an important part of the game."

Do you want to start a family?

"One day. But for now I'm just enjoying the journey. This sport is so selfish, the time and dedication you've got to put into it. When you get to the UFC, you think you're the shit and you know the game, but it's a whole new level, in every sense—the fights, the media, the fans."

So many fighters say they don't care about the belt, but I'm calling bullshit. How bad do you want it?

"[Laughs] It's true, you hear that a lot. Maybe it's because you don't want to set yourself up for a letdown. There are so many variables. If I tell myself that no matter what happens, I'm going to get that belt, then I get in a car wreck and can't fight again, then what? But I think about it. I do. The closer you get, it's like it pulls you in that direction, keeps stealing your attention. So you push it away, work harder. *I guess that's the irony.* I'm here to prove to myself that I'm the best fighter in the world, and getting the belt solidifies that. How else do you really know? You don't. You need the belt. But still, you have to stay focused on what's real, what you can control. I can control how hard I train, but I know the UFC could cut me tomorrow."

And Myles is correct. Joe Silva, matchmaker for the UFC, rarely gives interviews. Dana calls him Benjamin Button, or "the grumpiest old man in a young body you'll ever meet," but it may have something to do with his job description: he's tasked with pitting fighters in thrilling, title-relevant bouts, and should a fighter lose *too many* fights, Joe drops the axe. Question is, how does he define "too many"?

"The hardest part of my job is balancing sport and spectacle," Joe told me. "The fans want excitement, but there's the title contention, and some fighters are just flat-out boring.

"The worst part of my job is cutting fighters. Think about how hard it is to lose a job. But this is more than a job, this is a lifelong dream, and I'm the one that crushes that. Even if a fighter loses three in a row, inside he's telling himself, It's just a slump, three wins and I'll get a title shot, I can still win that belt."

Joe lifted a notepad from his pocket and scribbled some numbers. "Fans get upset when I cut a fighter, but look at these numbers. . ."

The UFC promotes 33 events a year.
@ 12 fights per card, and 24 fighters per event
that's 792 available slots

PROBLEM: UFC retains 450 fighters under contract
each owed 3 fights per year
that's 1350 needed slots

SOLUTION 1: promote 23 additional events (1 per week)
or
SOLUTION 2: cut 190 from the ranks

"We can't carry this many fighters. It's so damn expensive to put on an event—the travel costs, the advertising, the manpower—it stretches the company thin. And revenues? People don't realize that without pay-per-view buys, MMA doesn't work. Television networks don't pay enough—not yet at least—and the gate doesn't cover the costs. The sport is still growing. One day the ad revenues will cover, but we've still got a lot of work to get there."

It's not about the money, most fighters will parrot. And I somewhat believe them because as with most sports, in MMA only the most acclaimed athletes earn mansion and Bentley money. Oh, and don't forget recent reports that 78 percent of NFL athletes go broke within three years of retirement, and 60 percent of NBA players within five. So if it's not about the money, and if, let's say, a title shot remains a distant glimmer up the mountain, why do these mid-pack fighters continue clawing and stretching for a higher foothold?

"One of the reasons I got into fighting," Jon Fitch told me, "was because I'd never really been in a fight. It's like in *Fight Club*, the famous line, 'How much can you really know about yourself if you've never been in a fight?' Yeah, there were some minor scrapes at the bar, where one punch is thrown and it's broken up. But the opportunity to step into a cage with another guy, and the only way out is win or lose, now that's terrifying. But it was something I had to do, because how much do you really know about yourself without facing that fear? It's the clearest mirror you'll ever stand in front of."

Three days later, Jon Fitch lost a unanimous decision to Demian Maia at *UFC 156* in February 2013. Two weeks later, the axe fell, severing him from the UFC roster. Fans freaked, taking to Twitter and Internet forums to complain that the cut was unwarranted, unfair—but few crunched the numbers. Dana shrugged "It sucks, but welcome to sports. We've gotta trim the rosters so the guys remaining get the fights they're due."

—

A few days after sitting with Myles Jury, I'm in line at Keen's coffee (a local Newport Beach digs) and in walks Ian McCall, carrying his one-and-a-half-year-old daughter, London. Small world, this MMA. We chatted, watched London totter about the shop, petting a dog, and it hit me—Ian and Myles appear so different, but both fighters have sacrificed everything to climb that mountain. The only real difference is that Myles just left base camp, while Ian is near the peak.

McCall started training under Chuck Liddell during Liddell's zenith years. Training with, and partying with. But for McCall, the partying got out of hand: he suffered a near-lethal overdose and awoke days later in the hospital. He entered rehab, and, thankfully, saw the light. Now he's one of the top-ranked flyweights in the world. He's also a single father, changing diapers while working for that belt.

So tell me about the journey. . .

"I've always been a prodigy in the gym, but I liked drugs too much. It all started when [laughs]. . . No, seriously, I was wrestling in college, think I was eighteen and I'd already fought, when I hooked up with Chuck Liddell. We started training, and right off the bat, he told me—you're gonna be champ one day. Then I saw him grab the belt, and he blew up, became like a rock star overnight. It was insanity. I'll tell you right now, no one partied like Chuck. Not before, or since. Those years were off the rails. Unfortunately, that put the idea in my head that that lifestyle was okay. And for that I paid."

Well, it's not like you're the first.

"No. You're right. I've partied with rock stars, movie stars, and hands-down, fighters party the hardest. It's weird. I think it's because we are so tied to the gym, and so strict, and we have that agro gene that make us want to just freak out, so when we go off, it's not pretty. I'm not saying all fighters. Some never party. But me, before rehab, I liked excess way too much."

Does having your daughter help you stay straight?

"Very much so, because I know I can't fuck this up. I'm raising London on my own, and though it's hard, she makes life so good for me. It's exactly what I needed. I've done everything a man could want: traveled, partied, seen cool things, and when my girlfriend said she was pregnant, I was like, alright, I'm going to man up and do this, I'm going to try and earn money and provide a nice life for this little girl. It might sound cheesy, or cliché, but my mom used to say, I love you so much it hurts. I never knew what that meant. But now, with my daughter, I think about her when she's not with me, and the sadness—my mom was right, it hurts."

How much longer do you see yourself fighting?

"I'm twenty-nine now. For most people that's young, but for a fighter, my time is limited. I'm getting older. I'm strong, I'm fit, but training non-stop takes a toll. I'm not elastic anymore. I hope five more years. I've got to get that belt. Anyone in the know knows I'm better than Demetrious [Johnson] and Joe [Benavidez]. I haven't performed well in the UFC, and it's embarrassing."

Is that your motivation, fighting for the belt?

"There will be so much weight lifted when I win the title. I'll feel so much better about myself. Now, I feel like a failure. I came into the UFC to do a job, and [losing the flyweight semi-final to Demetrious Johnson] I failed at it miserably, and I can't live that down. It sucks. So now I'm in the gym all the time, but it's still never enough. I train so hard, but it's like I need complete world domination, you know? *I need to fuck shit up on a daily basis, or I'm not happy with myself.*"

What advice would you give a fighter just starting up the mountain?

"Stay sober and in the gym. I wish I had focused a little harder. Everything was so available to me, fun was so available to me, and early on I picked fun over training, and I regret that. So my advice: work hard, and don't ever take your eyes off the prize."

Wanderlei Silva.

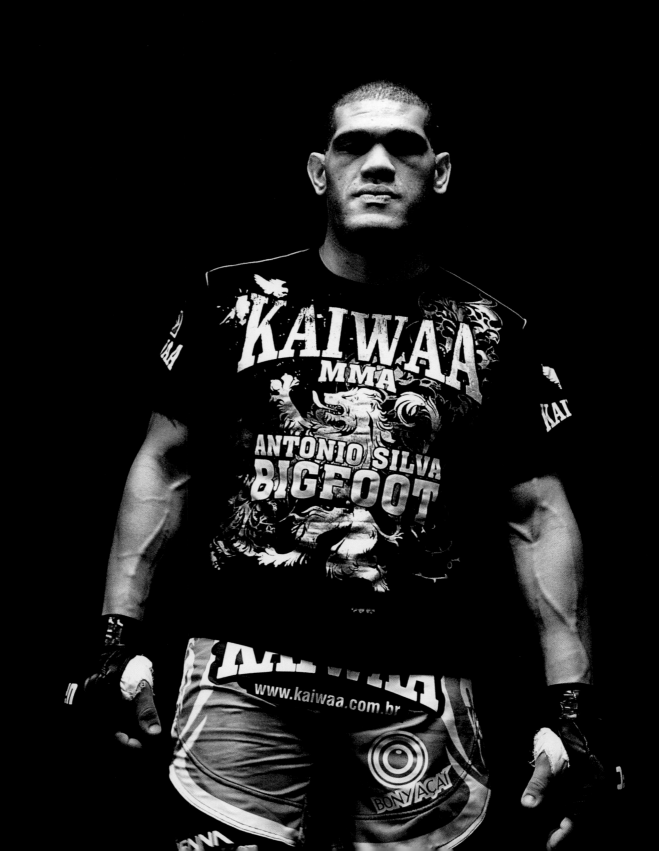

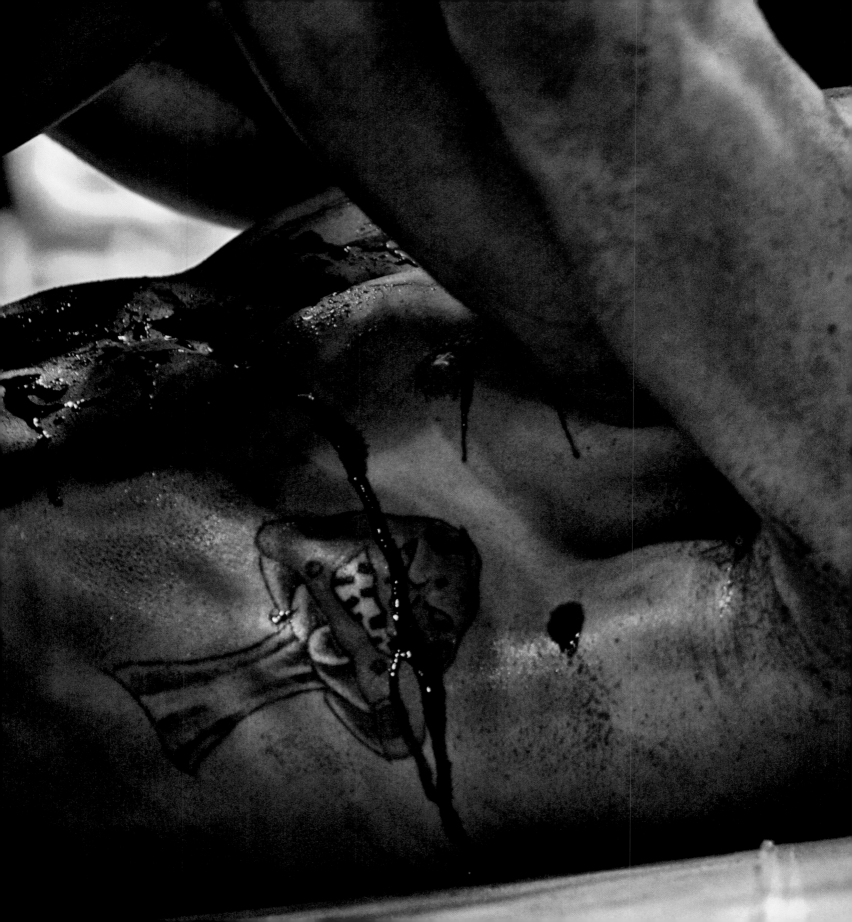

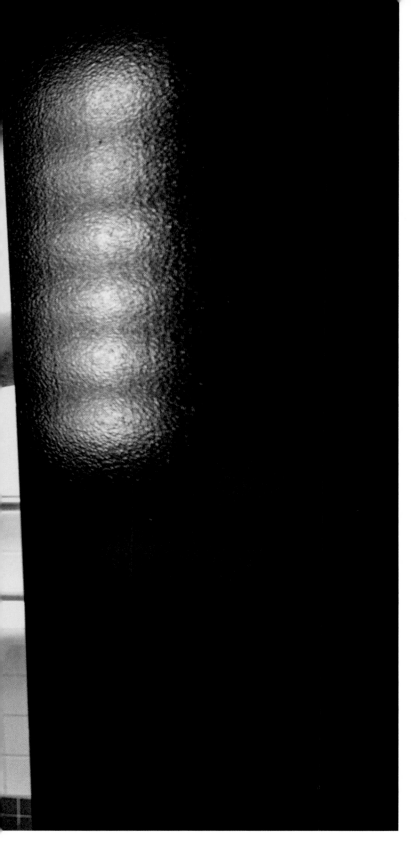

This page: Joe Lauzon mulls his loss to Jim Miller.
Previous pages:
1) Family portrait: Ian McCall and daughter London. (Painting by Matt Gordon.)
2) Antonio "Big Foot" Silva.
3) Lance Benoist defeats Matt Riddle.
4) Darren Elkins post-win.
5) Jiu-jitsu, the soul of MMA: Myles Jury and Rafael Mendes.
6) Top: Ariel Helwani interviews Cung Le backstage; bottom: Alistair Overeem.
7) Top: "Rampage" Jackson; bottom: Jake Ellenberg.

8: HEAVY IS THE CROWN

"Uneasy lies the head that wears a crown."
—WILLIAM SHAKESPEARE, *HENRY IV*

A FIGHTER STEPS INTO THE CAGE, the crowd chanting, his walkout song thundering through the arena, and ten minutes later he's disoriented, gripping the fence, struggling to right the world. A fighter steps from a limo, waves to fans and cameras, and ninety minutes later he ducks a right hook, throws a wild left that allows a knee to the chin—this fighter, after years of sacrifice and hardship, finally earns his shot, so for two grueling months he trains six days a week, six hours a day—jiu-jitsu, boxing, muay Thai—and on the appointed day he checks into his hotel, and next thing a pen light is flashing in his eyes while he begs the referee, "No, don't, don't stop it, I'm okay, I'm okay!"

But it's over, this fight, his dream of a title, one hundred eighty-three seconds and now trainers, league officials, camera crews pour into the cage. A bloody glove cradles his neck. The champion hugs this man, this challenger, and kisses his forehead, then the champ steps to the microphone, and Joe Rogan's questions go unheard amid the cheers. Staring over the camera, forget about what our champion is supposed to say, because what he's thinking is, *These pay-per-view numbers better kill it, 'cause I'm getting that pad in Miami* [and] *oh damn, those girls in the third row, let's get this over with before the arena clears, 'cause I got this suite till Monday . . .*

"I'd just like to thank my coaches and team," the champ carefully says because he's learned that even the slightest misstep spawns a headline, and with every title defense the spotlight brightens—

Uneasy lies the head that wears a crown.

On November 12, 2011, MMA was thrust from the shadows and into the blinding sun. Since *UFC 30* in February 2001, the first ragtag event after the Zuffa acquisition, Dana

Georges St-Pierre in the tunnel.

dreamed that one day, who cares if he didn't have a PPV deal and who cares if his current productions sucked, one day a major network would broadcast the UFC like the NFL, and millions would watch . . . Of course he never uttered such a thing beyond closed doors because, hey, not even Nevada would sanction an MMA event, but they'll see, one day—

Twelve years later, the day came, and when it did (via *UFC on Fox 1*), we were packed in an SUV, driving to the arena in Anaheim, California, for the event's heavyweight title fight between Cain Velasquez and Junior dos Santos, broadcast live on Fox Network—yes, home of the Super Bowl and *The Simpsons*. Dana stared out the tinted window at the looming Honda Center. "Bro, I can't believe it. We've been working toward this for so long, it feels like a dream."

A month earlier, to announce the historic partnership, a cadre of UFC and Fox brass filed into the broadcast studios: Dana White, Lorenzo Fertitta, David Hill, Eric Shanks, Joe Rogan, Rashad Evans, Chuck Liddell, Frankie Edgar, Georges St-Pierre.

"This [sport] is going to get bigger, and bigger, and bigger," David Hill, Fox Sports guru and industry titan, told the cameras. "This is just the beginning. I can't overemphasize the way this sport has gone from niche to mainstream in just ten years . . ."

But there is no yin without yang, and the increased publicity ratcheted up the pressure.

Night of the fight: Dana paces the dressing room, texting with one hand, while speaking to a reporter on the couch. A news crew sets up lights. Caterers arrange food trays on the table. He leans close and shows me his assistant's iPhone screen: "Look at this, over fourteen million fans tweeted about the fight. The ratings should fucking kill."

Three hours later: the arena is packed. Bruce Buffer announces champion Cain and challenger JDS. The ref signals. The fighters shuffle to the center, and slowly circle, feeling the distance. Cain throws a lazy kick. Junior answers with a jab. First dance jitters, and more than any other weight class this pitter-patter is warranted because when a heavyweight cracks you in the skull, good night.

Hands raised, Cain presses forward, trying to engage the elusive JDS, and as the tension builds—*something's gotta happen, right? I mean, come on, these are two of the baddest motherfuckers on the planet*—JDS lunges an overhand right—and understand, I've stood next to the guy, his hands are mallets hanging from thick branches, and at six-foot-four and 240, forget the metaphors, he swings and connects, it's over—JDS lunges that overhand right. Cain collapses. Junior leaps atop him and drops more shots. The ref pushes him off. And at just 1:04 of the first round, the fight's over.

That's it?!

All the hype, all the billboards lining the 405, all the press releases and media events. Done in sixty-four seconds.

Kneeling cageside with the other photographers I glance around. Half the arena cheers, the rest cover their mouths, gasping. A Fox producer, seated next to Rogan, rolls his eyes.

Thirty minutes later: Dana again paces the dressing room, only now, "That was the worst fucking possible outcome. Fuck. The guy's a world-class wrestler, why the hell's he trying to box!"

A week later, not so bad: six million homes in the United States watched the broadcast, along with another twenty-two million in Brazil.

Welcome to the Brave New World. A world with more media, more scrutiny, more wagging fingers, more reasons to think long and hard before you speak or tweet or act. In this new world, by the time a fighter scales the mountain and seizes the belt from that pinnacle, he or she has given countless interviews and seen his or her answers twisted, cherry-picked, and reassembled, so now he or she is a black belt in regurgitating soundbites for hours all while revealing nothing . . .

Uneasy lies the head that wears a crown.

The Stare-down: Nate Diaz vs. Benson Henderson.

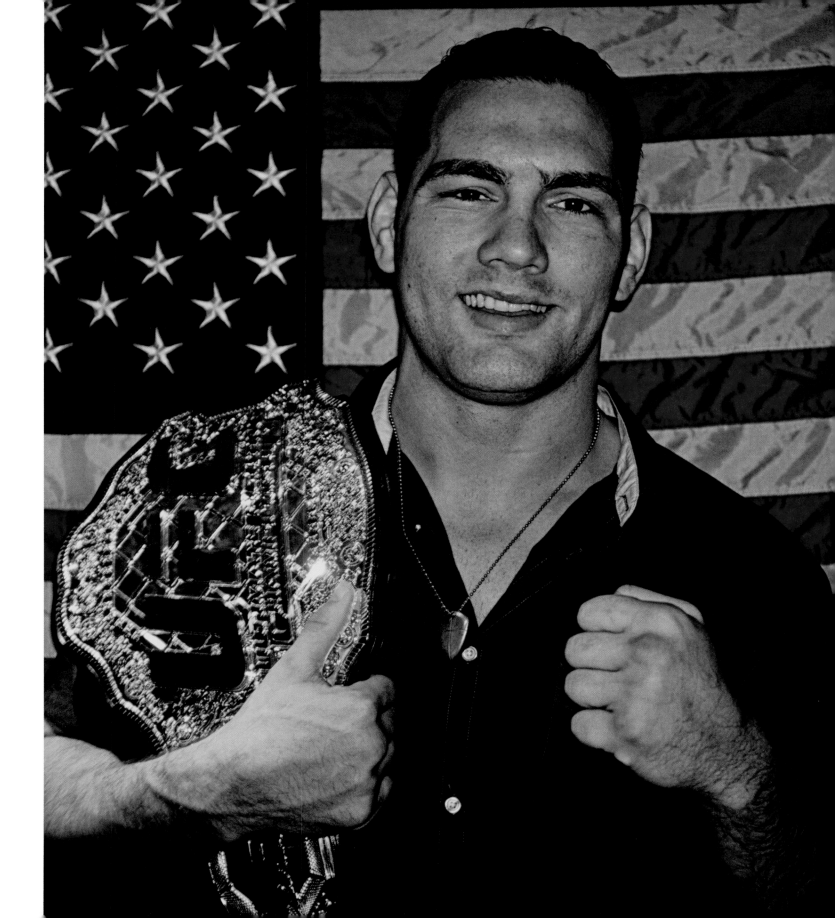

—

Georges St-Pierre: "I don't like doing [media interviews] . . . no seriously, I despise it . . . I like you guys, but I don't like doing this . . . it's not you I don't like, it's that—basically, people who know me, I've been repeating the same thing fifty times every week, it's like a computer in my head: *bap bap bap* . . . I don't like it, but it's part of my job, I have to do it. Every job is not perfect."

Frankie Edgar: "I try not to think about it—I just want to win the next fight because that takes care of everything. It sounds simple, but it is simple. If you try to put too much pressure on winning, you get overwhelmed . . . of course I fight to be number one, and when you get that belt it's like, we did it, but it's not about the recognition. I'm a private kind of guy. It's really about the feeling: after you train so hard, and it all comes together, you knock a guy out or earn a hard-fought win, it's that satisfaction."

Vitor Belfort: "Of course my goal is to get another shot at the championship and train [a full camp] for it. When I fought Anderson I trained, but with Jon Jones I was a replacement—it wasn't my championship. I prepared as much as I could, and what's crazy, I had the fight in my hands, I was winning, I had the chance to take it, but I made mistakes. After a long career I still make mistakes, so my focus now is just to have fun and finish stronger than I started."

Ronda Rousey: "I don't feel any different fighting for the title because losing at anything, even sparring, inside feels like dying, like the end of the world. When I was twelve and lost the finals of the Junior [Judo] Nationals, I locked myself in my bedroom for a week and barely ate. Whether it's a high school gym or millions watching pay-per-view, I hate to lose."

B.J. Penn: "When I won that first belt, it happened so fast and so easy, I could not believe it. Before then I fought ten full rounds for the lightweight title and lost both fights, and here I win the fucking welterweight title in just two minutes. It didn't feel real. I remember Dana putting the belt around me, I was like, I'm never taking this off, I'll sleep with it every night . . . but a couple days later I didn't look at it again. That's the way things are. After winning the belt I thought, That's it, my whole life's done, I will never have to accomplish another thing. So funny. I actually looked at the belts more this last month than I have in my whole life, because with the kids I've been hanging around my mom's house more, and that's where I keep them."

Rory MacDonald: "I'm ready to be champion. My skill set is there; now it's just a matter of experience. I'll fight anyone."

Benson Henderson: "I don't think about the pressure. I've always treated every fight like it was for the title. And that helps. First time on the main card, first time as the main event, first time on Fox—there's always another first with even more pressure, so you have to just train and fight. I want to be the best, so I have to fight the best and beat the best. It's that simple."

Previous pages:
1) Benson Henderson vs. Nate Diaz.
2) Chris Weidman, outside his hotel room half an hour after his historic defeat of Anderson Silva.
3) GSP, "The Gladiator."
4) Renan Barão, enjoying the view.
5) Junior Dos Santos.
6) Jon Jones shoulders the weight.

Opposite: Cain Velasquez backstage, warming up.

9: WOMEN'S MMA

"How important it is for us to recognize and celebrate our heroes and she-roes!"

—MAYA ANGELOU

No way. Never. Not a chance in f—— hell. For years, this was Dana White's position on promoting a female fight in the UFC. Yet, on December 6, 2012, during a press conference in Seattle for the *Fox 5* card, Dana signaled Ronda up to the podium and handed her a shimmering UFC championship belt—crowning her champion of the newly formed and vacant UFC women's division.

So just what erased Dana's line in the sand?

Some fans point to the *ESPN* magazine cover "The Body Issue" and its nude photo of Ronda swiveling toward the camera, fists encased in pink boxing wraps. Others say, No, watch her fights, she's a beast, most guys couldn't hang. But for me the answer came three months prior, the night I hurried into Mr. Chow, a Los Angeles bistro, and rushing through the tables I saw Dana White and, *holy shit,* Ronda Rousey.

Of course I knew her from interviews, websites, mingling at events, even watched her playful banter with Conan O'Brien—but I didn't *know* know her. So I'm thinking, *Dana, bro, dinner with Ronda Rousey for my birthday, how cool is that?*

I pulled up a chair, clueless this was the dinner at which Dana would break the good news, and with all the charm I could summon, I flashed my gap-toothed grin her way.

"Yeah, I know he looks homeless," Dana said, chopping my game at the knees. "But he's my homie, and he lost his tooth—"

Great, the story. Most people either ignore the gap or some, the fearless few, flinch and finger their own grill before asking. As Dana rehashed the tale, Ronda sat with hands in lap, slack-jawed and glancing my way every few seconds. A good sign I should signal the waiter for drink.

Ronda on set.

"Fucking nuts, huh?" Dana grinned.

Ronda nodded.

"Uh, so how about that weird interview," I blurted, trying to deflect—and what I meant was, that week a video had hit the Internet in which the reporter completely crossed the line with Ronda. "Your presence is, uh, amazing . . ." the guy said, "the attention you, uh, pay to the moment, makes my life, like, so much more fun right now . . ."

Ronda gazed at the ground, *Is this dude really hitting on me?* she seemed to think.

"That guy was weird as hell, right?" I said.

"Hold on." Dana raised his palm. "Now I know that was strange, but I'm gonna defend the guy. It's *that thing*—she's got that thing that just sucks you in, and you can't turn away."

Dana is a promoter, and though he'd sworn up and down that no way, never, would women fight in the UFC, once he met her, once he saw how fans reacted to her interviews and fights, who was he to deny?

That was the answer—she had *that thing.*

After Dana broke the news during dinner at Mr. Chow, we head to the *Sons of Anarchy (SOA)* season 5 premiere in Westwood, California, where Ronda would first meet the media as part of the UFC family.

These nights are always a big deal. Hollywood studios need to hype their marquee shows and rope viewers into the new season, so the marketing engines redline to promote the premieres. And for *SOA*, FX network's ratings darling, they roll out the red carpet.

We pull up to the theater. Spotlights roam the sky. Fans lean over barricades, calling to Ron Perlman, Kim Coates. The driver stops and we spill out.

"Yo, homie!" Theo Rossi rushes up and hugs Dana. They pose for pictures, and I drift to the side and wonder how the random attention must feel—personally reaffirming, or like living in a glass bottle, where every compliment echoes like the last. *Oh man, Dana, I love what you've done for MMA . . . Theo, I've never missed an episode . . . Ronda, I can't believe it's really you, is there any way, I know you get this all the time, but is there any way I can get a picture?*

Flashbulbs pop. The paparazzi scream, *Ronda! Ronda!*, for the moment ignoring Ryan Hurst, Charlie Hunnam, even Dana. To gauge a star's wattage, on the red carpet just compare how often the paparazzi yell for their attention. *Here! Ronda! No, here, over here!*

—

Inside the cavernous theater I cram next to UFC fighter Brendan Schaub, who's crammed next to fighter Shane Carwin. Shit flows downhill, so when Shane muscles Brendan for room, he muscles me. Hardly the birthday snuggle I was hoping for.

Kurt Sutter takes the stage. The bespectacled ponytailed creator of *SOA* thanks his cast and crew, wife Katy Seagal, and so on. The crowd cheers. The lights dim, and if you're a fan of the show, you know the premiere is intense—so intense that during the final scene I nearly vomit prawns and walnuts onto Schaub's blazer.

I watch through laced fingers. Dana's shaking his head, and Ronda, she's holding her mouth in shock. Which is ironic, the queen of arm-snapping grossed out by this bit of fiction.

Just two years prior Ronda entered her first amateur MMA bout. It was quick work. The ref signaled go and after a quick tussle she gripped Hayden Munoz's arm between her thighs, and torquing the limb straight, then a few degrees into the pain zone, she forced the tap. No cageside onlookers would realize it at the time, but this submission would define her career. Over the next two years Ronda faced an impressive array of challengers, and she made swift work of them all.

11/12/2010 Autumn Richardson Round 1 0:57 seconds Armbar

01/07/2011 Taylor Stratford Round 1 0:24 seconds Armbar

03/27/2011 Ediene Gomes Round 1 0:25 seconds Armbar

06/17/2011 Charmaine Tweet Round 1 0:49 seconds Armbar

08/12/2011 Sarah D'Aleio Round 1 0:25 seconds Armbar

11/18/2011 Julia Budd Round 1 0:39 seconds Armbar

03/03/2012 Meisha Tate Round 1 4:27 seconds Armbar

08/18/2012 Sarah Kaufman Round 1 0:54 seconds Armbar

02/23/2013 Liz Carmouche Round 1 4:49 seconds Armbar

If you want real-world intense, watch the video of Ronda dismembering Meisha Tate's arm—back arched, tweaking the elbow until the skin whitens, ready to *pop!* Now that will turn your stomach; it was so intense that fans nominated it the "2012 Submission of the Year."

If all this sweaty grappling and bone-breaking seems rather "un-girlish," realize that Ronda was raised in a dojo, climbing gym bars, sitting matside while mom (Ann Maria Rousey DeMars) swept the '84 World Judo Championships, becoming the first American to earn gold.

Those are big shoes to fill, especially when Mom also earned several post-judoka academic degrees. With the trophies, medals, M.B.A., M.A., and Ph.D. diplomas on the walls, there was scant room for dolls in this house. But it was Dad, Ron Rousey, not Mom, who dreamt of seeing Ronda on the Olympic podium, and it was Dad who shuttled her to practices and swimming meets—that's right, our future hero started in the swimming pool, not the dojo.

Then her world imploded. At just eight years old. Standing atop a snow-packed hill, she watched her father's sled race down the path, careen, and plow into a snowbank.

Top: Ronda warms up under the watch of Manny Gamburyan.
Bottom: Ronda Rousey versus Liz Carmouche.

The soft snow shrouded a log, and though he walked away from the crash, the damage to his back prompted doctors to insert a steel rod to stabilize the injury. Nevertheless, his spine began deteriorating, and doctors next gave him a terminal sentence: in just a year he would lose the use of his legs, then his entire body, and within two years the deterioration would kill him. Always active, so involved with his daughters, he didn't want them to forever carry the image of him wasting away in a hospital bed. So he took his life, and Ronda's rock, her *mentor*, her daddy, was gone.

Of course she was devastated, and when she turned ten, to channel that grief, Mom started her in judo. "The gym was far from the house," Ronda said, "so to make the drive worthwhile she'd make me roll not only in the kids' class but also with the adults. I started tournaments a year later."

Thus, the journey started—training, competing, training, competing—and at seventeen the wunderkind qualified for the 2004 Olympic Games, then won the World Junior Judo Championships, and earned a bronze at the Junior World Championships, which, for most of us, hell yeah, pop the champagne corks—but not Ronda. "My mom never praised me once—" she shrugged "—after I won the bronze medal, she said she was disappointed."

Who knows, perhaps this denial of praise and the constant pressure molded her into one of the best female judokans to ever grace the mat, but the little girl in her suffered. "I know people view me as this tough-ass chick," she told me, "but I cry. I cry a lot. Every single night from thirteen to eighteen, after training I'd be in the locker room sobbing. I needed to be perfect and beat everybody in the room. If anybody threw me even once, my God, it was so painful. I never cry from an injury, but if someone threw me, I'd bawl."

Top: Ronda backstage before receiving the first women's UFC belt. Bottom: morning workout.

The path to the Olympic podium was rocky and strewn with thorns, and halfway there, the week of her eighteenth birthday, she ran away from home. "With my mother and coaches always pushing, pushing, there wasn't a moment in the day for me. Every moment, every second other people planned, I had no say. I didn't have the courage to confront them. My way of standing up for myself was to buy a plane ticket and fly across the country. I went to my friend's house in Albany."

In time she began training again, and "to pay the bills I entered tournaments, and I swore, to show everyone up, this would be the best year of my career. That's why I moved to Montreal . . . but once I got there, no one would coach me because I was American. Judo culture is total bullshit like that. But this only pushed me harder, and training on my own I won the World Cup, medaled three times in Europe, and, sure enough, everyone wanted to work with me again. So I went back, hoping things would be different, but after I medaled [earning bronze at the 2008 Olympic Games], not one coach or teammate called to see if I got off the plane in L.A. safely. It's like, Oh, we're done with her now. They didn't give a shit. These were very superficial relationships, and that left me very angry and spiteful, so I decided that's it with judo, I'm done."

After mulling what next, she transitioned to mixed martial arts, and who would've guessed that in this more vicious world she would find the camaraderie, acceptance, and love she always craved. She finally found home. "Now, my coaches and teammates are my best friends. God, I'm so glad I'm not in [judo] anymore. I couldn't even watch a full match in the Olympics last summer."

Ronda entered the cage six times in a single year; for a bit of context, during 2012 Jon Jones fought twice. Just flip through her 2010–11 slideshow: each time she walks out note the background, and how in each photo the crowd grows: more cameras, more cellphones recording her passage, more fans reaching for just a touch. "When I first moved to Los Angeles I was so poor I lived in a dirty little apartment, waiting tables at Gladstones by night, training all day, and now—"

Now she walks down the sidewalk and moms stop her, clasp her hand, and thank her for serving as a role model. Make no mistake, Ronda is *the* poster girl for women's MMA. The icon who inspires females around the world to hit mitts, kick bags, don *gis*. Everywhere you turn: That slender teller at the bank, chipper smile and bruises on her forearms, she trains MMA. The flight attendant clicking shut those overhead bins, she trains. Ottavia Bourdain, wife of revered chef Anthony Bourdain, and Amanda Lucas, daughter of George Lucas, creator of *Star Wars*.

As does Taylor Ross, an eleven-year-old surfer girl from Orange County, California.

TAYLOR ROSS

I first heard of Taylor through her work with Pipeline to a Cure, a charity that aids those afflicted with cystic fibrosis (CF). The charity seeks to marshal the surfing world to help with fundraising and public awareness campaigns, and here's the surf connection—CF is a genetic disease that triggers thick mucus buildup in the lungs. Doctors realized that inhaling saltwater mist, via frequent swims in the ocean, reduces inflammation and infection.

The surfing community is small, so a friend tells a friend of my interest in MMA, and next thing my phone rings. "Bro, you gotta come see this little girl, she surfs down at Blackies and she also fights. She beats on boys, it's awesome."

That week, after watching YouTube videos featuring Taylor's fights, I drove to an office park in Costa Mesa, and strolling into OC Kickboxing & Mixed Martial Arts, a gang of kids in white *gis* ran past. It was a typical MMA gym: a small weight area near the boxing ring, Helio Gracie photo and inspirational posters on the wall. But walking to the back, I saw three rows of kids, thirty in all, patiently awaiting instruction, and just as many soccer moms seated along the mats, sipping Starbucks, casually chatting.

That's when I realize it's not just men and women training MMA—it's also our kids. Welcome to UFC Nation.

In the second row a little girl, with streaked blond hair and blue eyes turns and waves at her mom. It's Taylor, and it's such a touching moment I melt. Partly because I know Taylor's disease is sapping her health, yet she's so cute, always smiling. And when you learn the median age for those born with CF is thirty-seven—and that's median, not guaranteed—you want to hug her, or punch a wall, or both.

Back in the UFC offices I told Dana about Taylor, and moved by her commitment to spread awareness of the fatal disease, he picked up the phone and in minutes a small team joined us around the conference table. The next week a crew from *UFC Ultimate Insider*, a weekly show on Fuel TV, descended on her gym. Filmed her training, interviewed her family at home, then we went surfing. "I wanted to start jiu-jitsu after I saw the *Karate Kid*," Taylor told the cameras. "I can relieve stress by taking someone down. Sometimes I think of the disease when I hit the bags."

THE AFTER-PARTY

Following the *Sons of Anarchy* premiere, we head to Gladstones, a restaurant overlooking the moonlit Malibu beaches, for the after-party. It's more of the same: *SOA* cast and crew, industry execs, paparazzi. Dana stops to chat with Charlie Hunnam, and I follow Ronda through the crowd, to a bar tucked far from the racket. Turns out she knows the layout well, as this is where she used to wait tables.

She peers over my shoulder, trying to spot the manager, who she says treated the servers badly, and I'm curious

Taylor Ross shadow-boxing.

about this need to show others up—her old judo coaches, this manager, her mom. Because if the will to win is an elite athlete's greatest weapon, perhaps she consciously nurses these slights and snubs, stoking the fire, anything to power through another training session.

We order drinks, me another shot, her water, and sit in a booth and chat.

So what do you think of these studies that show women earn 77 percent as much as men for the same work?

She shrugs. "Well, it's better than it used to be, but still it's a process. Even in sports. A guy walks into a gym, his reputation precedes him—if he's won in the Olympics, that's never questioned. But me, when I walk into a new gym, I have to prove myself over and over again, because everyone's questioning whether I'm *really* that good."

Do you like watching women's MMA?

"Yeah, those girls throw down. It's very rare you see a boring women's MMA match, it seems they always have a chip on their shoulder, something to prove. And they're newer in competition, so they're less structured in the way they fight. You never know what's going to happen, all bets are off. Not like the calculated matches you see on the men's side. Women take it personal. They leave the ring still angry, like ring the bell again. They want it more than boys."

Do you recommend MMA for young girls?

"Sports are a metaphor for life. Training and competing builds confidence. Girls shouldn't have to walk around afraid. I carry myself differently knowing that whatever happens, I can handle it. That confidence translates into whatever I do. Like the other day I was at a media lunch, surrounded by journalists. Years ago I would've been intimidated, nervous, but I tell myself, Well, at least I can beat the shit out of anyone in this room. Crazy, but that confidence calms you, even

Top: Stitch wraps Taylor's hands backstage.
Bottom: Taylor and Ronda.

if it's not relevant to the situation. You carry yourself differently, and that's something a lot of women lack."

That's the take-away?

"Yeah, that and learning to delay gratification. Everything is so instant now—you instantly get food, instantly talk to people, instantly fly to an exotic island. But competing requires so much dedication, so much time and effort, it's the best way for kids to learn discipline. You can't sit a five-year-old down and tell them the importance of college—that's too far away. But you can put them in a *gi* and push them onto the mat, let them learn and practice moves again and again, let them experience the rewards of hard work."

Are you glad your mom pushed you so hard?

"Yeah, now I am. When I was younger, as a teenager, I thought my mom was trying to ruin my world, making me go to camp morning and night. I never went to a slumber party, a dance, or anything like that in high school. I was training. But now the sacrifice is paying off, so I'm glad. And if I can inspire other girls, it was worth it. Most girls don't have a world champ walking around the house like I did, and that showed me that anything was possible. If I can provide that to anyone else, that would be awesome."

UFC FOX 4: SHOGUN VS. VERA

The *Ultimate Insider* shoot culminated at the Staples Center, in Los Angeles, in August 2012. I met Taylor and her father as they entered the arena, and like any first-timer at a UFC event, Taylor was awestruck by the crowd, the mega screens simulcasting the action inside the Octagon, the fighters walking out to pumping music, the postfight interviews in the cage.

But it was also Taylor's night: the cameras captured her eating popcorn and licorice, pointing out celebrities in the crowd. Then I led them backstage, past the production crews and into the locker rooms, where she watched fighter warmups and even spoke with Joe Lauzon and Brandon Vera. In the hallway, Stitch taped her hand as though she were prepping for her own bout.

Then she met Dana, and the way he broke from a production meeting, shifted gears, knelt and spoke with her—it's a rare gift to connect with all walks and ages, and not every corporate exec possesses this innate skill. Taylor handed Dana a shirt, which he unfolded and laughed as he read, "You can't handle the tooth!"

After the backstage tour, near the cage she spotted Ronda. I introduced them, and as they posed for a picture, this wasn't just girl meeting woman, this was disciple meeting one who'd already scaled the mountain.

———

I should confess, before starting this book, I too opposed women's MMA. I couldn't imagine watching females slug and kick each other. But after meeting Ronda, and watching other elite female fighters, I began to see the light. Ronda Rousey and Meisha Tate coached *The Ultimate Fighter* season 18, and the show featured women and men contestants. During the season 18 tryouts, I walked into the waiting area and stood among more than seventy female fighters. That's when I realized: these women, and girls like Taylor, sacrifice and suffer just as much as any man. So who cares what the hell I think—this is their sport, not mine. If I don't like it, I can change the channel.

Postscript: Four months after the *UFC Fox 4* event, a bacterial infection spread through Taylor's lungs. Her parents rushed her to the hospital, and after lengthy tests doctors gave her a 50 percent chance of survival. It's not the liver disease, or the painful blockage of pancreatic ducts, or the scarring of the lungs, but infection that accounts for most CF casualties. Thankfully, Taylor beat the odds and, at least for now, she's back in the gym, and in the water.

Ottavia Bourdain rolls with Renato Laranja.
Following page: Ronda Rousey grapples with B.J. Penn while the Mendes brothers look on.

IO: *THE ULTIMATE FIGHTER (TUF)*

"Do you want to be a fucking fighter?!"
—UFC PRESIDENT DANA WHITE

DANA STORMED INTO THE WAREHOUSE a few miles from the Vegas Strip, unsure of how to handle the crisis. "Things were fucked. My back was against the wall. Four years of my life on the plane twice a week, never seeing my family, working sixteen hours a day, even Sundays, and it was all crumbling around me."

To say the stakes were high is an understatement: if this first season of *The Ultimate Fighter* reality TV series flopped, as most first-season reality shows do, who knows what the hell next, maybe back to training clients, or promoting local boxing bouts, or even schlepping luggage as a hotel bellman. "Walking into the gym I was so angry my hands were shaking. I thought I was going to puke. Ten million, that's all I was thinking, ten million to put on a show about fighting and now the fighters didn't want to fight . . . what the fuck! I had no idea what I'd say, and when I lined them up, it's not like I was rubbing my hands, thinking, Oh, this is a great speech moment—"

Let's recap with a quick slideshow: (*circa* 2000) On the phone Dana tells Lorenzo the UFC is on the blocks . . . inside the Trump Plaza arena (*circa* 2004), a slew of empty seats and near the cage Dana grips his cell, brow creased while he receives news that the event is on track for a dismal 40,000 PPV buys . . . Dana at a year-end accounting meeting (*circa* 2005), unconsciously covering his mouth while projected on the wall a red line zags across four years, every fiscal quarter a loser . . .

They'd hired the best, spent millions on advertising and creative promotions, yet none of it increased the PPV revenue. Which meant the losses piled up. *UFC 1* garnered 80,000 PPV buys, *UFC 2* got 300,000 buys, and over a decade later, despite state sanctioning, advancements in techniques and training, numerous national ad campaigns, piles of news stories and magazine covers, the latest event yielded a paltry 40,000 buys.

Come 2008, my family's road trip finally wound into Vegas, and after Dana picked me up we head to the Fashion Show, a mall on The Strip. Over pizza and salad at CPK we caught up, and recounting how bad things got, he said, "We all grew up together, right, so imagine I talked you into buying this thing, and your family's against it, but you do it anyway. Then it starts tanking. Every quarter the same story, all while the casinos are also taking a hit. Everyone's shaking their heads, wondering why you jumped in with me, the dude that got kicked out of Gorman [high school]. And I'm coming into your office month after month, telling you, 'Bro, I know you're hurting, but we need more.' It was depressing. For the last infusion [of cash] Lorenzo was so ashamed he didn't even ask Frank for his half, just funded it himself. Finally, Lorenzo broke and told me to sell it. That was the worst night of my life . . ."

In 2004, the Fertitta brothers found themselves in a blood-soaked ER, the casinos hobbled, the UFC on life support. That summer they'd launched *American Casino*, a reality TV series crafted to market their new Green Valley Ranch property. The show drove traffic to the resort, increased awareness more than any campaign, and that success lit the bulb: *Damn, if this worked for a casino, why don't we rent a house and fill it with young fighters, who bet your ass in close quarters will bicker and brawl, then we'll match them to fight in the Octagon . . .*

No brainer, right? Sixteen adrenalized fighters vying for a lucrative UFC contract. Just add water, step back, and film the mayhem.

Stoked on the concept, Lorenzo and Dana flew to Hollywood and pitched every network in town. *Listen, forget Survivor, our show is more intense and cheaper to produce, it's called* The Ultimate Fighter *. . . Meeting after meeting, each and every pitch ended with polite handshakes and a Thanks, guys, love your enthusiasm, BUT American audiences will never buy into a new sport.*

Michael Chiesa weighs in.

They learned quick that Hollywood execs are all racing for second place. Forget innovation, the strategy is to clone a proven winner, tinker a bit here, change the title from *American Idol* to *X Factor*, then rush it to market—hence all the copycat reality shows. Who cares if *Big Brother*, with its similar stuck-in-the-house concept, worked. Or if *American Chopper*, another niche concept, worked. Thanks, but no thanks.

This was it. Lorenzo and Frank met behind closed doors, deciding how to unload the money pit. Again, Dana waited. Hours passed. The phone rang. Dana answered, expecting dire news; instead they offered to personally front the $10 million in production costs.

Long story short: Producers auditioned and filled the house with hungry fighters, Chuck Liddell and Randy Couture agreed to coach the teams, Spike TV agreed to air the episodes, and just weeks into production, Dana received the call that a handful of fighters were complaining about cutting weight, and well, they didn't want to fight.

So Dana marched into the *TUF* gym, head buzzing with finances, friendship, family, and as he scanned the gathered fighters—including Forrest Griffin, Chris Leben, Josh Koscheck, Stephan Bonnar, Kenny Florian—he realized this wasn't just his great opportunity, but also theirs, *If I was their age, in this place, with so much on the line, all this national exposure—*

"Do you want to be a fighter?" he asked. "That's the question. It's not about cutting weight, it's not about living in a fucking house, it's about, *Do you want to be a fighter?* It's not all fucking signing autographs and banging broads when you get out of here. It's not. It's no fucking fun, man. It's a job, just like any other job. So the question is not did you think you had to make weight, did you think you had to do this . . . [it's] *do you want to be a fucking fighter?!* That is my fucking question, and only you know

The Apostles, Mike Rio and Daron Cruickshank.

that—anybody who says they don't, I don't fucking want you here, and I'll throw you the fuck out of this gym so fucking fast your head will spin. It's up to you. I don't care . . . cool? I love you all, that's why you're here. Have a good night, gentlemen."

During the storied episode, the screen cuts to Chris Leben, who summarizes: "The famous fucking fighter speech. Someone should get him an Emmy for that one." He laughs, then sobers. "It fired me up, it was intense, you know, here I am coming from fighting in only small shows, and now I've got the president of the UFC asking me if I want to be a fucking fighter or not, so it definitely lit a fire underneath it."

Forget the Emmy and crafting MMA lore, this was war. Each week following the January 17, 2005, premiere, Dana paced the office, waiting for the ratings. Thankfully, with each episode the audience grew, and come *UFC 51* on February 9, 2005, the PPV buys rebounded to 105,000. Which signaled a heartbeat. The patient gasping. But don't pop the champagne yet—

Throughout each *TUF* season, sixteen fighters compete, every week eliminating two more via two-round bouts until only the finalists remain. Every season culminates with *The Ultimate Fighter Finale*, and that first finale, broadcast live and free April 9, 2005, featured Stephan Bonnar versus Forrest Griffin.

Make or break, this was it. The last hurrah. Fans inside the Cox Pavilion, located on the University of Nevada, Las Vegas campus, had no idea they were soon to witness history. Bruce Buffer announced the fight. The ref dropped his hand. Griffin and Bonnar rushed across the cage, and it was on—a non-stop slugfest that brought the crowd to its feet; and throughout the bout Joe Rogan exclaiming, "This is a battle here . . . what a war . . . that first round was the Hagler–Hearns of MMA . . . these guys are swinging . . . this

Top: Urijah Faber.
Bottom: Jonathan Brookins coaches Michael Chiesa.

crowd's going nuts . . . the craziest war I've ever seen . . . I'm just honored to be here watching this . . . [and finally] how do you call anybody a winner in that fight?"

Afterward, bruised and panting, the two fighters stood, heads bowed, between referee Herb Dean. Bruce Buffer announced the scores: 29–28, 29–28, 29–28 . . . winner by unanimous decision . . . Forrest Griffin!

Dana handed over the glass plaque, announced the new car, the new motorcycle, then told Stephan Bonnar that he was no loser, the throw-down also earned him a six-figure UFC contract.

The next morning Dana paced that familiar trench in his office carpet, glancing at the phone on his desk, *Where the hell are the overnight ratings?!* Ring. He leapt over the desk and, holding his breath: 3.3 million viewers.

Holy shit, this can't be right.

Dana hung up the phone, and right then it rang again, and again, and again, all day, reporters calling for comment. "That was the greatest fight in UFC history," he gushed, more relieved than boasting, because he knew, Yeah, great ratings for a free-TV audience, but the company lives or dies via PPV buys. PPV buys—and in just a week would come the true test: *UFC 52*, *TUF* coaches' finale, pitting Randy Couture against Chuck Liddell for the light heavyweight belt. Would even a fraction of that massive audience make the leap?

Well, the next Saturday the dam burst, and after that event's record-breaking 280,000 buys, prayers answered, the well-watered fields ceded their bounty, and Dana never had to ask for another infusion.

—

A few months after Michael Chiesa slammed Al Iaquinta, slid behind, and caught him in a rear-naked choke, winning season 15 of *The Ultimate Fighter*, we caught up backstage in Seattle. "There's no way I could ever prepare myself for winning the show," he said. "It's like a catapult that throws

you from watching the UFC at home on TV to sitting in the front row of the arena. It still blows me away."

Like Alice down the rabbit hole?

"Hah, yeah, it's crazy, the strangest thing was learning to make peace with my new life. I worked so hard, so long, to get here—then, when you make it to the other side, it's trippy. Before everything was such a grind, now every morning I just get up and train. I don't have to worry about money, or go punch a clock. Now fighting is my job. It's my life. I never would've imagined, but that's been a major adjustment."

You feeling the pressure?

"Of course. *TUF* produced world champions Forrest Griffin and Rashad Evans, so yeah, I know everyone's watching. I just tell myself, One fight at a time. Forget the rest. Of course I want the belt, and I want to take advantage of the opportunities, but I'm gonna take the toughest fights and work my way up."

How was that first day back in the gym?

"It's heavy because now everyone's out to get you. You go from up-and-comer to the guy with a target on your back. I didn't see that coming. After winning the show guys want to hurt you so they can go home and say, 'Oh yeah, I beat the crap out of Mike Chiesa today.' They're like, 'Screw this UFC guy, I'm gonna take his head off.' So now I have to perform in every training session. That's hard when you're pushing through camp, dog tired, and left and right guys are gunning for you. But I was the same way. One of my best friends is Cody McKenzie [*TUF* season 12 competitor], and when he came off the show I was like, 'Oh, I can't wait to get my hands on him, I'm gonna beat his ass.' I'm just as guilty."

Previous pages:
Top: Master Thong warms up Daron Cruickshank before his *TUF* bout; bottom: Andy Ogle consoles Jon Cofer after a loss.
Top: Michael Vick removing his "lucky" handwraps; bottom: Team Cruz, group prayer.
This page: Michael Chiesa submits Al Iaquinta for the *TUF* crown.

II: THE MACHINE

THE UFC IS *not* a fight company, it's a production company—one of the biggest in the world—that just happens to sell fights. This is important, so I'll write it again: the UFC is *not* a fight company, it's a production company.

Yes, true, but with that logic you'd argue that Nike was a shoe company. Which it isn't. Sure, you can stroll through a Nike store and fill your basket with shoes and cleats, socks and sandals—but don't forget the T-shirts, pants, headphones, golf clubs, that wireless watch, and those shorts and sunglasses. Forget shoes, Nike is the world's largest advertising agency, but it didn't start that way.

It's fascinating to identify the parallels between the two companies: the engine under Nike runs on advertising while the UFC is fueled via production.

In 1964, Phil Knight and Bill Bowerman stood on the University of Oregon track field while runners sprinted past. Bowerman ripped apart a heavy cleat, standard for the day, and told Knight, "Dude, this shoe sucks, we can make these damn things lighter, more comfortable"—and as the legend goes, Nike was born.

In 2000, Dana, Lorenzo, and Frank attended an early UFC event in New Orleans, and glancing around at the half-empty arena told each other, "We can do this so much better . . ."

Thirteen years later, Nike asked Dana to speak at their corporate gathering in Las Vegas. "In the early days, cable networks wouldn't carry MMA, but they had no problem with porn," Dana said. "Now we're broadcast in 145 countries around the world, into 350 million homes."

Ha ha, funny *now*, but this bias forced the young company to learn film and television production. They didn't want to but circumstances forced their hand. Just as Knight and Bowerman intended only to build a better cleat, but soon found themselves brainstorming slogans, shooting arty photos for ads, writing commercials, courting famous directors.

Top: Anderson Silva selling the fight.
Bottom: Chael Sonnen at the public workouts.

Typical fight promoter duties involve selecting venues, negotiating fighter contracts, speaking at press conferences; but Dana found his days consumed with writing commercials, giving notes on promos, and crafting storylines, while at events he directed camera angles and reviewed every walkout song. Some might call this micromanaging, but if anything angered fans or offended advertisers, Dana alone answered the call.

Start an advertising agency, and, no question, my first choice for president would be Phil Knight. Start a production company, and I'd choose Dana White. This is what rival fight leagues don't grasp—it's not just about finding a talking head. The Craigslist job posting for promoter should read:

Help wanted promoting MMA fights.
Comfortable speaking in public before thousands of fans, journalists, and television cameras? Have the ability to corral the egos of the toughest men and women on the planet? Here, there, so many fires and things-to-do you'll sleep a mere three, four hours per night—but, hey, what's health when you're flying around the world on a private jet! :-) Oh, and the right candidate MUST understand all aspects of video broadcast and production, so if you fit the bill, apply here!

In addition to *The Ultimate Fighter* reality TV series, UFC produces *UFC Ultimate Insider*, *UFC Tonight*, *UFC Primetime*, along with several YouTube blogs. That's millions of eyeballs glued to the revolution.

BEHIND THE CURTAIN

To understand a company, any company, we must plunge through the skin and bones and locate its beating heart. Forget org charts. Forget titles. Those only obscure. Instead, seek out the company's core competency, the thing no competitors can match. Again, consider Nike: the swaths

of accountants, lawyers, engineers, assembly-line workers, even the athletes—these are merely cyborg limbs dependent on that life-giving pulse. No world-class advertising = no sales = no contracts = no fall season = no new product = no endorsement money.

So if *I* were to profile Nike operations, I'd march past the reception desk and down that long hallway lined with classic posters, past the conference room, and rounding a corner I'd bust in on the head of advertising; and as she picked up the phone to call security, *Ma'am, wait, please put that down, I know so few recognize the real game here, it's just commercials, right, she's just hawking goods, we hold the purse strings . . . but I see where the true power lies . . .*

At UFC headquarters, if you walk through the entrance lobby and up the stairs, past reception desks you will reach the office of the executive vice president of production, Craig Borsari. And just how do we know this is the right door? Because it's the only entrance adjacent to D.W.'s. To wit, the old adage: *proximity = power*.

As Dana's right hand, Craig oversees every aspect of production, including prepackaged and live events. Those stirring *Primetime* segments. Those exciting pre-fight commercials, same. Every pay-per-view broadcast. That's why Dana spends half the day in his lieutenant's office, reviewing edits and mapping strategy.

THE WHEEL

Lorenzo Fertitta describes UFC events as the hub of a wheel, with the connected spokes representing ancillary products. It's an apt analogy because fans watch the fights, then fill their carts with shirts, programs, necklaces, training bags, action figures, gloves, video games, magazines, etc.

Top: Craig Borsari, pre-fight production.
Bottom: Mike Goldberg and Joe Rogan.

So we've got a wheel spinning 365, powered by this production engine . . . a machine with five-hundred-plus employees around the globe, and the control room nestled in the Zuffa corporate offices, a few miles off the famed Vegas Strip.

SELLING THE FIGHT

Everyone has a job: editors edit, accountants balance, lawyers argue, and fighters, well, they sell the fight. Sure, there's training and dieting and climbing the mountain, but if you want the fame and glory and the money, then you gotta *sell*, with a capital *S*.

"It's not enough to win," Dana tells fighters. "You've gotta make an impact."

Translation #1: Build your brand.

Translation #2: Study the writings of Carl Jung.

In the book *The Hero and the Outlaw: Building Extraordinary Brands Through the Power of Archetypes*, authors Margaret Mark and Carol Pearson profile companies as diverse as Nike and Marlboro to illustrate the importance of leveraging ancient archetypes in order to pierce the white noise of mass culture and thus "make an impact."

Sure, you must win, but ever wonder why some fighters get numerous title shots while others don't?

Answer: Archetypes.

Consider: GSP, the white knight. Anderson Silva, the wizard. Nick Diaz, the anti-hero. Chael Sonnen, the trickster. Ronda Rousey, the huntress.

If I were a fighter I'd leave nothing to chance. I'd study the interviews and videos of break-out fighters, and note how each reinforces their archetype: GSP trains harder than any mortal. Anderson Silva's style defies convention, and he moves (as per Stephan Bonnar) like someone from *The Matrix*. Nick Diaz misses press conferences and flips the bird at cameras. Chael Sonnen calls out an entire nation, then on television licks Rashad Evans's shoe.

But aligning with that archetype is only the first step; next, for each and every fight you must build the rivalry.

RIVALRIES

Fight fans incessantly debate the GOAT (Greatest Of All Time). *Not even a question, Sugar Ray Robinson . . . bullshit, Roy Jones Jr. in his prime was untouchable . . . are you crazy, what about Willie Pep?!*

It's an ageless argument without answer. But there's no disputing the all-time fight salesman was Muhammad Ali. *The Greatest* sold a fight like none other. It's sheer genius how he turned every opponent, even close friend Joe Frazier, into an arch-enemy because he knew that nothing sells tickets like the prospect of a fierce rivalry.

Few MMA rivalries compare with Ali versus Frazier, Madison Square Garden, March 1971. Imagine the nerves, the excitement, in witnessing Ali's first fight after being stripped of the belt for protesting the Vietnam draft. Christened "Fight of the Century," what's most tragic is that no matter what we do, rewatch the tapes, interview eyewitnesses, we'll never truly appreciate the energy of this, or any, all-time rivalry unfolding in real-time. The verbal jousts. The put-downs. If I could power up my time machine, I'd first *zap* back to 1954 and watch Helio Gracie versus Masahiko Kimura, at Maracanã Stadium, Rio de Janeiro, October 1951 . . . then I'd *zap* to Ali versus Frazier . . . then to Chuck Liddell versus Tito Ortiz, Mandalay Events Center, Las Vegas, April 2004.

Thankfully I was there for every moment of Anderson Silva versus Chael Sonnen, MGM Garden Arena, July 2012.

During the hoopla, I sat with Chael and we talked about the game.

Tell me about promoting a fight. [Chael is the greatest fight promoter in the UFC.]

"I don't know much about promotion. I don't have an interest in promotion. I am purely an athlete."

As a kid, were you introverted or extroverted?

"I don't know . . . where I lived, in the middle of nowhere [West Linn, Oregon], nobody had cable TV, cell phones. There was no such thing as the internet. You spent a lot of time alone, playing and finding ways to occupy the time. So I guess that qualifies as an introvert."

When you started dealing with the media, promoting your MMA fights, was it difficult, or did you just jump right in?

"The sport grew around me—it's still growing. I don't do a whole lot of interviews. I'll do one, and it gets picked up and recycled on every site, often my quotes changed."

Does that aspect of the MMA media—the same questions, and the "tweak and reposts"— frustrate you?

"I find it comical. It's certainly bizarre and unique to this industry."

At what point in your career did you decide to say whatever it takes to get under your opponent's skin?

"I never had thoughts like that. But there was a point when I decided to just answer things honestly. I went through the whole fake thing for a while—every fighter does—where you answer the questions according to protocol. But then I realized, you can't be afraid to pick a fight when you're in the fight business. I'm glad I did it, it was refreshing. I tell others, don't say something about a guy just to say it. I was very angry at Koscheck after his fight with GSP. Kos built this fight up for a couple of months, in the ring [after the fight] he said, hey I didn't mean any of that, I was just promoting this fight. Well, that's called fraud. You can't say anything to sell something that is not true. Tyson did it after the Lennox Lewis fight, after losing he says, 'Oh, this is a great guy.' People accuse me of the same thing, but I would never ever manufacture conflict. I don't talk trash, I talk truth."

You ran for political office [State Representative in Oregon's House District 37]. What's the parallel with fighting?

"They are both campaigns—it's all about getting your message out there. Why would someone tune into my fight if there is another fight out there? That's my job, to campaign for their attention. Politics sucks, and so does fighting."

Why do you say fighting sucks?

"It's difficult and grueling. There is only a small percent of the population that will raise their hand and sign up for this. It takes a unique person."

Do you find it ironic that in the fight game they deal with a simple scenario, X versus Y, and try and complicate the issues; while in the political game they take very complex issues, and try and oversimplify them?

"I completely agree. So funny. Guys go off to camp to prepare for a fight, and they act like they are leaving for university to study nuclear science. Why you need a camp to learn how to punch is beyond me. Why you need seclusion to know you have to run three miles in under fifteen minutes is beyond me. It's the strangest thing. I love boxing guys that sit around with their gold teeth and try to break down a fight—look at this guy's footwork, his range and movement. All of that is made up. There is no such thing as footwork, range and movement. It's just two guys fighting. Yeah, they move their feet, and yeah, there's a range—but in the end, it's just two guys in a cage. Doesn't get any simpler."

Will you run for political office again?

"I'd like to. We've got a real dirtbag in office from my district. There are few things more frustrating than Congress raising good hard-working people's taxes—when half these [politicians] don't even pay their own taxes. It's the ultimate irony.

"My motivation for running is to represent good people. It's not a job that I want to do, it's a job I'm willing to do."

How does political campaigning differ from fight promotion?

"They are both very difficult, and unique. With campaigning you go house to house. People slam the door, kick you off their property. The same thing happens in the fight world—there's a lot of negativity when you are out there promoting. It's just part of it."

Previous pages: UFC ambassador Chuck Liddell, at a regional Orange County MMA bout; Dana White in studio; Arianny Celeste at the *TUF* Wall of Fame.

Following pages: weigh-in mayhem; countdown, Chael backstage with Mike Dolce; Chael on deck; Sonnen vs. Silva II; Chael backstage after loss; Dos Santos and Silva celebrating; reconciliation—true martial artists; Dana counselling Chael immediately after fight.

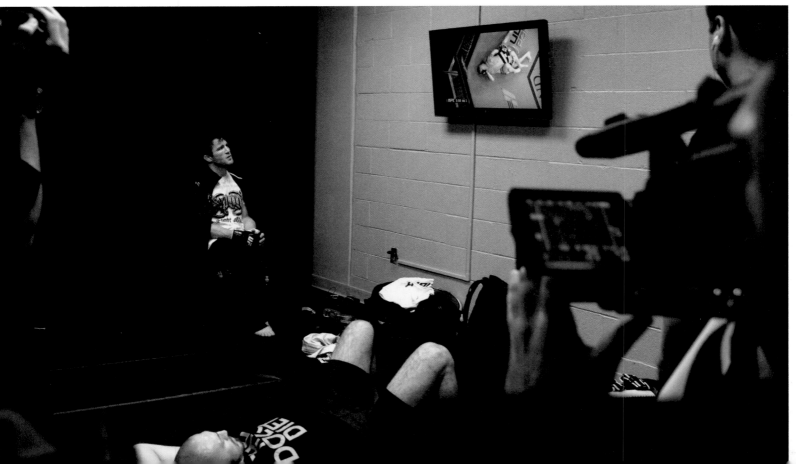

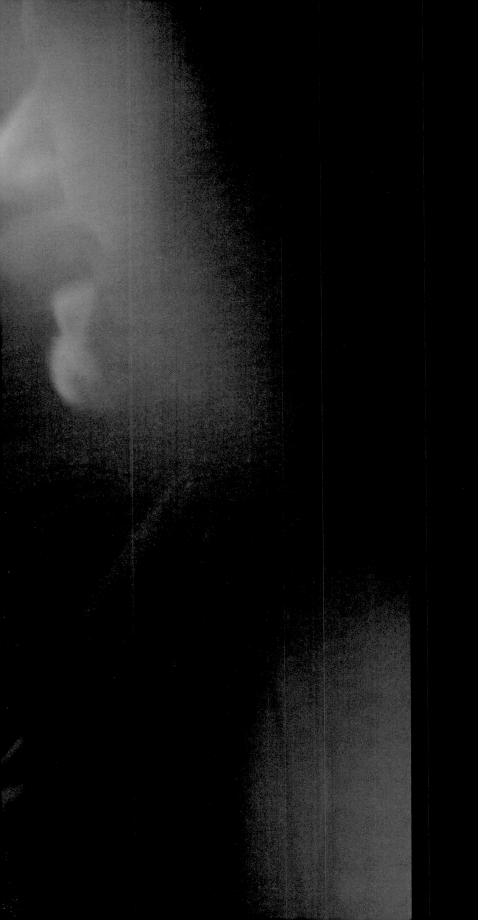

12: JOE ROGAN

AFTER FINALIZING THE UFC PURCHASE, Dana White returned from New York and in his office stood amongst the assets of his newly acquired company—eight tattered cardboard boxes. He tore back a lid, rifled through stacks of dusty VHS tapes, and popped in a cassette. As he laid out faded brochures and wrinkled T-shirts, the entire day and into the night he watched prior events.

At some point, perhaps while propping a championship belt atop his bookcase, he heard laughter. On the screen: comedian Keenan Ivory Wayans, elbows on knees, leaned in his plush chair and asked a talk-show guest how Steven Seagal might fare against a real-world MMA fighter. The screen cut to Joe Rogan, who, snorting and waving his hands, showed just how a fighter would grab the actor's greasy ponytail and *Bam! Bam! Bam!* beat him senseless.

Dana cracked up, and returning his attention to the belt, *Damn, this thing looks good up here,* he reflected on the fights he'd just watched; there was something missing. *What the hell was it?* Not the fights—he'd seen some barn-burners. Not the cheesy graphics, or the synth music—they were already on the "got to go" list . . . *Shit, that's it!*

This is when I like to think the ceiling tore asunder, and raising his hand to block the fiery light, in a road-to-Damascus vision Dana glimpsed the UFC in its present glory: an overflowing arena, the crowd chanting and seated alongside the Octagon, hunched over a microphone, the powerful Joe Rogan.

Listen up, son, this is not your parents' fucking sport!

I know, it's ridiculous, the atheist struck with a heavenly vision. But the point is, when Dana swore to overhaul the whole package, he knew he needed a transformative figure—not a fighter per se, but a ringside archetype to entertain and inform viewers. Fuck the suit and tie or, worse, tuxedo-wearing commentators. Who set the sports broadcaster cum Brooks Brothers trend? Fake. Fake. Fake.

Joe Rogan and Duncan Trussell.

No, this new-era fight league needed Joe Rogan, the *Fear Factor* host who was willing, on a national broadcast, to mock the most recognized martial arts actor in the world.

After making countless calls Dana finally reached Joe. "I told him we'd just bought the UFC, and I wanted him ringside, calling the fights. 'I don't have any money, I can't pay you,' I said, 'but if you can just hang in there, when this thing takes off—'"

Joe agreed to hitch his horse to the ragtag caravan, and over the next few years he commentated ten, twelve events *por nada.* "Now, whatever Rogan wants, Rogan gets," Dana says. "Without him, fuck, I don't even want to think about it."

Say what you want about Rogan, he lives and breathes martial arts. Training and competing since he was a kid, at nineteen he won the U.S. Open of tae kwon do. After high school he left the dojo for a career in stand-up comedy, which led to a role on the sitcom *NewsRadio.* But his love of the fight never waned. In 1997 he conducted backstage interviews for the prior UFC owners, and he now holds a black belt in jiu-jitsu.

It's difficult to overstate Rogan's impact. If Dana White is the pope of this new religion, then Joe Rogan is its archbishop. Fighters enter the cathedral, and fighters depart, and some never to return. But there Joe stands, announcing their passage.

—

The night of my first UFC fight I followed the entourage to the Mandalay Bay for an official after-party. At the door a bouncer waved us inside. I pushed through the crowd, trying not to fall behind, up the stairs to a booth overlooking the floor. Screens on every wall flashed Dana's photo. He was hosting this get-together—which, I didn't realize, he'd never done before and never would again.

Living on the beach in rural Florida, I hadn't set foot in a club in eight years. The slinky dresses, the thumping bass. What a trip. I downed a few shots, and staring out at the dance floor, I realized people were staring back.

Did I spill nachos down my shirt? Is there something wrong with my hair?

I look beside me, and, oh shit, there was Joe Rogan, just chilling.

Dana strolled up, rapped a bit with Joe, then he grabbed my neck and asked if everything was cool. Joe watched the exchange, and when Dana walked off, he gave me the nod.

"Hey—" I offered my hand, about as awkward as if I'd just wandered down from the Appalachian Mountains "—I'm a huge fan, glad to meet you."

"Cool. So how do you guys know each other?"

"We grew up together."

He tilted his head, as if to say: *Really. If you grew up together, then why the fuck, in seven years, have we never met?*

"Yeah, this is my first fight," I admitted.

Long pause. His head tilted a bit further.

"Uh, I was in Florida."

—

Not long after that night, Rogan debuted *The Joe Rogan Experience*, a bi-weekly podcast. That was about the time I started this project, and trying to learn everything about this new world, I decided to jump down the Rogan rabbit hole, and follow the trail, no matter how thorny, or how strange.

When Rogan advocated jiu-jitsu training, I started grappling. When he claimed that sensory deprivation tanks expanded consciousness, I floated. When his comedian buddies, a.k.a. The Deathsquad, appeared on the podcast, I attended their stand-up gigs. And when he touted "the fleshlight," a faux flashlight that when unscrewed revealed a silicone vagina, well—

Whoa, whoa, whoa, that's way too much information, you say—and dammit, what the hell does a bizarro podcast have to do with the UFC?

Well, everything.

When Dana vowed to recraft the sport into something so kick-ass thrilling fans couldn't help but flock, he banked not only on Rogan's encyclopedic fight knowledge but also on his *Fear Factor* audacity, and the nothing-is-off-limits approach of his stand-up comedy. So the last thing he'd do is throw a wet blanket on him.

But the pressure is mounting. During the maiden Fox Broadcast, Dana and Rogan stood before the cameras, shouting and preaching the word to this wider-than-ever audience, while in their earpieces a Fox producer urged Rogan to calm down.

"What the fuck, that's how he always acts," Dana later groused in the dressing room, "he gets me all fired up, and that's why I brought him on board in the first place. Fuck that. We're not changing a thing."

Let Rogan be Rogan—it's the same punk rock ethos that Dana embraced in his youth. Why he still wears Dead Kennedys and Misfits T-shirts. Yet, in these latter days, it's not just pressure from Fox—it's also internal.

Growth, stress, adaptation—it's a relentless cycle—and as the company grows to five-hundred-plus employees, with recruits arriving daily, more often than not this fresh talent hails from Fortune 500 companies and Ivy League schools. Which makes sense. Hire the best. Hire proven winners. And task them with protecting the brand.

And herein lies the schism: for eight years the brand was forged by a T-shirt-wearing bald maniac who shouted fuck across public podiums, cursed during interviews, and even behind company doors. For example, when executive meetings denigrated into unproductive yap-fests, which is standard fare for any corporate environment, Dana would point across the table and yell: "Shut the fuck up! Just shut the fuck up and don't say another fucking word! You're talking stupid and I don't want to hear any more!"

Protect the brand?

Gotta love that. Let's not forget Rogan, whose typical podcast tenets include:

1. Legalize Cannabis
2. Psychedelic Excursions

3. All Things MMA
4. Bigfoot might/might not exist
5. Government Conspiracies
6. Stand-up Comedy
7. Don't Act Like an Asshole
8. Computer Simulation Theory—i.e., the world as we perceive it is not real; as in *The Matrix,* we're all living in a virtual program

It's a mad fusion, and every week the sect grows. In fact, it's so popular that in summer 2013, the SyFy channel began airing Question Everything, a cable show hosted by Rogan, which incorporates elements of the podcast.

Then there's the stand-up. Most Friday nights before the fights, Rogan performs at a club in the host city. After announcing the gigs on the podcast, then tweeting to a million-plus followers, the tickets usually sell out in minutes. Gone. Just as gone as the days of traditional marketing, where, in these host cities, morning of the shows he used to make the rounds and pump the gigs on local radio stations. Now his disciples travel the country, following the UFC cavalcade like post-millennia Grateful Deadheads.

—

So what's Rogan really like?

That's a question I'm often asked. I've grubbed with Rogan, watched boxing bouts in the arena dressing rooms with him, seen his stand-up countless times, chilled on-set during several of his podcasts, even hung backstage with the Deathsquad before one by one they stepped on-stage.

Understand, my backstage m.o. is always fly-on-wall: sit in the corner, contribute nothing, keep the camera low until they've forgotten I'm there. When you listen to the podcast, or better yet, watch the proceedings live, you get the feeling that Rogan and guests are hanging out in a basement, smoking pot, shooting the shit. And that's a

fairly accurate summation. Same with the comedy shows. Prior to a gig, Rogan and his cohorts hang in a back room and await their stage calls. Seated against the wall, I was surprised by how much this resembled the backstage UFC locker rooms before a fight. The pre-war tension, the nervous laughter, the small talk—anything to prep for those ten, fifteen minutes under the lights.

There's also the pecking order. Anthony Pettis, Lavar Johnson, Cung Le, Frankie Edgar—they all might share the same locker room, but when Anderson Silva strolls through the door, they stop and watch the master pass.

Same with the comedians. Joe leads the conversation and they follow.

So what's Rogan really like?

Standing amongst the toughest men on the planet, or comics who every night endure unruly drunks and hecklers, Rogan is *the* Alpha Male.

Here's their backstage exchange: Rogan leans near Duncan Trussel, a fedora-wearing hippie, and whispers something I don't catch. Duncan responds in a high-pitched lesbian voice (his words, not mine)—and typing this now, I'd like to reach back and let Duncan know his left testicle is stricken with cancer, so enjoy it while you can, buddy, because in eight weeks a surgeon's gonna slice that lil guy out like a rotting walnut.

Joey Diaz, a heavy-set Cuban with a Bronx accent, announces that he's volunteering as coach for a youth basketball team.

Ari Shaffir, a lanky bearded Jew sitting cross-legged on a chair, says he'd like to volunteer and give back, "… it's gotta feel good, right?"

"Yeah, but you sit like that," Rogan quips, "and some kid's gonna point at you and say, 'Daddy, I don't know about that man.'"

Diaz howls. "Hah, but those long legs are perfect for triangles. Mechanical advantage is everything."

With these guys there's no segue, just *bap! bap! bap!* so now we're on to MMA.

Ari: "Yeah, how 'bout that Stephen Struve."

Rogan: "Jon Jones."

Duncan: "Nick Diaz."

Diaz rubs his belly. "Oh man, no more steak and eggs for me, that meat was still alive."

There's a long lull as we, at least *I*, envision a bloody ribeye lodged in his cavernous intestines.

"I just had a meeting with this production company," Rogan says, "they want to film a TV show; bring in scientists, challenge Bigfoot claims, shit like that."

Everyone nods. No shock here. Hollywood comics, such as they are, spend late nights in comedy clubs, and early mornings at casting calls, hoping, praying for a television gig to pay the bills. But Rogan's got the Midas touch. *Of course* when he wades into the digital landscape he's so successful his stand-up career rockets through the atmosphere, and now he's killing it with Onnit—an Internet company that sells fringe nutritional supplements, kettle bells, blenders, medicine balls, protein bars, sea salt, raw killer bee honey—to listeners. So *of course* a production company wants to film a show around the podcast.

Rogan leans for a view of the stage. "I love this room because these same people show up every week, and that forces you to work on new shit."

Beyond fate or even divine providence, what he's hinting at is really the true explanation behind the "mad fusion"—it's really a closed-loop *fission* reaction in which UFC events feed the podcast which feeds the stand-up which feeds Onnit which feeds the fans . . . and now, at this club, The Ice House in Pasadena, the same crowd shows up every week after week, so they've heard each comic's routine more than once, which is what he means by, "forces you to work on new shit."

"Yeah, and they're super supportive here," Ari says.

Redban waddles through the curtain, wiping sweat from his neck. As the producer of all Deathsquad podcasts, he handles logistics and tech (computers, microphones, Internet connection, etc.). Rogan clasps his hand, then ducks through the curtain, and as with any fighter heading into the arena, I grab my camera and follow.

Equal parts hysterical domestic insights, mind-bending suppositions, and aggressive outbursts, Rogan's routine recalls the best UFC fights. Gay marriage, time travel, his young daughters, breast implants, masturbation—nothing is off limits—but when he talks MMA, miming Brock Lesnar grabbing hold of a guy and raping him . . . my camera drops.

The routine is no longer funny. That's when I realize, as the sport matures, and everywhere it's UFC billboards and UFC commercials, and as the arenas grow and the events take root in Madison Square Garden, Dallas Cowboys stadium, India, China, Russia, just as that scale tips and everyone you know is connected in some way to MMA, the UFC will face its greatest existential crisis as not one, but *two* charismatic leaders leave the cathedral.

Fold and highlight this page. Peering into my crystal ball, I promise you, five, ten years at most, fans will reflect all dew-eyed on this golden age, when despite the success and acceptance, there still lingered whiffs of the mad *fusion* that launched the UFC.

Soon, as with every other major sport's league, a suit-and-tie commissioner will preside over every press conference, and never will he utter a four-letter word. And soon, a suit-and-tie announcer will commentate every fight, and never will he wave his arms and shout at the camera.

There will never be another Dana, and there will never be another Rogan. So while this sunset remains golden, Ponyboy, stop and suck at that fresh air.

Now suck again.

Top: Rogan and Dana during the podcast.

Bottom: Joe and Dana.

Top: The Deathsquad.

Bottom: Rogan doing stand-up.

Joe Rogan prepping to intro the fighters, *Ultimate Fight Night 25.*

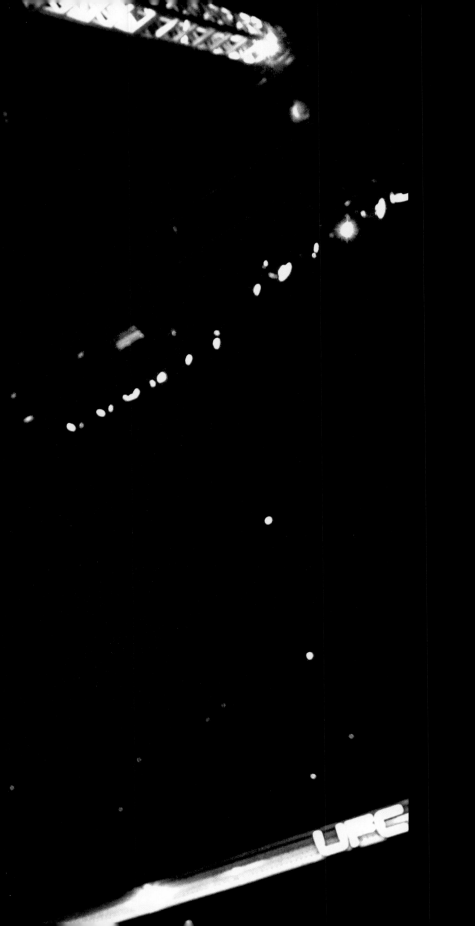

13: DANA WHITE

"Oh, shit. You're friends with Dana White? Just one question, I promise—what's the deal with . . ."

—ANONYMOUS UFC FAN(S)

OPPRESSIVE HEAT. CARS JAMMED ON THE STRIP. Tourists crowding the sidewalks and lined up outside the bars and restaurants. For those of us raised in Vegas, July 4th is a nightmare. Time to book that vacation, unless, of course, it's International Fight Week, the UFC extravaganza that featured the multi-day Fan Expo and culminated with the mega-rematch of Anderson Silva versus Chael Sonnen.

To court the media, the PR department booked a private cabana overlooking the Wynn Casino pool. Reporters filed in, sat under umbrellas and asked Dana their questions, then filed out. Next. Next. Next. This is called selling the fight, and if you're on the sidelines it's about as fun as, I don't know, answering the same questions over and over.

Then a Canadian reporter dropped on the couch and after a few tired questions asked Dana how he made new friends. Which evoked a pause. "I'm not looking for any new friends. This dude—" he nodded my way "—me and this dude have been friends since we were twelve years old. A lot of the people that I hang around with are the people that I've been friends with since I was a kid."

Which brings us to—

Question 1: Has Success Changed Dana?

You wouldn't believe how often I hear this one. For good reason. Fame, money, it's the American Dream, and yet we secretly wonder if its fulfillment corrupts. On Joe Rogan's podcast (#247), Tito Ortiz complained, "[Dana's] a different man. Totally different. He's not the same person. That's not Dana . . . I love him, I miss his friendship. Me

Dana White, moments before addressing the world.

and him were boys. I've seen him change . . . he's become, uh, he's become famous."

"Well, I've known Dana from the beginning," Joe responded, "from when they first bought the organization, he's definitely different. He's more confident now, he's more successful. But me and him, we have a very different relationship—"

Tito laughed. "When I was growing up they called that cockiness, but you said confidence—"

"But that hubris is how he gets things done," Joe replied. "That's why he's so good at what he does. He's got a whole lot of Don't Give a Fuck, and I appreciate that . . . I like watching people grow . . . I think you have to have an unflappable belief in yourself to run a company like that. You can say that's negative all you want, but I think, in order to do what he does, he's the guy for the job."

As a long-time friend, I'll second Joe on that: yes, of course he's changed. There's no equilibrium in a changing environment, and that's just the fucking way of the world. Job pressure, marriage, children, triumphs, failures, professional acclaim, personal rejection—every stress influences and forces adaptation.

Evolve or weaken and perish.

Yet, our friendship hasn't changed. Take last year, bored senseless in a hotel room, after arguing about what I can't remember, we started wrestling. Knocking over chairs, plowing into the wall. Finally, he grabbed hold of my collar and choked me until the room dimmed and Marty Cordova shoved him off.

Or this other night, at a club, I'm mesmerized by the troupe of pint-sized Oompa Loompas—and I mean little people with green hair, orange skin, white overalls—dancing and cavorting onstage. Big Bird peeked from behind the red curtain, and whatever this was, this mad burlesque, I couldn't get enough. Until a chunk of ice hit my neck. I glanced back, and Dana's standing on a booth, glass in hand, smirking. A trumpet blared. The Oompa Loompas tossed bowling pins. Another cold pellet slid down my shirt. I flipped him the bird.

Then another chunk hit me, the last . . . because I stormed over the seat and tackled him off the booth. For a moment time froze, the strobe lights blinding white, and suspended parallel to the floor, time engaged and we crashed through the table, shattering glass and splintering wood.

Nothing has changed.

"A friend is the guy that no matter what you did," Dana told the Canadian reporter, "no matter what's going on in your life, no matter what you have, you can pick up that phone and can call him and he's got your back."

Chuck Liddell rubbed his face when I recounted Tito's on-air comment. "I've been close with Dana for twelve years," he sighed. "I'm a fighter, but that doesn't keep us from being friends. Some guys just don't know what that really means."

Question 2: Why Do You Go to So Many Fights?

Traveling to UFC events week after week, month after month, for more than a decade takes its toll. The road is a lonely hectic grind. No matter how nice the hotel room, it ain't home. Ask any traveling salesperson or business consultant—the family misses you, the kids weep for your return.

So, for many events, to help break up the monotony, I'll jump on the plane and join the crew. There are usually five of us: Dana; Elliot Howard, video blogger; Craig Borsari, executive VP of production; and Marty Cordova, 1995 American League Rookie of the Year.

Marty, Dana, and I have been friends since we were teenagers. And nothing stokes us more than the others' success. Flashback to '95: Dana lay on the couch after a hard day at the gym, and thumbing the remote, flipping through the channels, on ESPN he read the breaking news: "Marty Cordova Breaks Minnesota Twins Record for Consecutive Homeruns."

Dana with the Fertitta brothers.

He leapt up and screamed, "Holy shit, he fucking did it! He did it!"

Though we'd moved on, each following paths beyond the Vegas valley, we kept tabs. I own Marty Cordova baseball cards, signed balls, action figures. Every few years we'd reconnect over dinner and drinks; but neither time nor distance diminished that stoke. I'd track his stats in magazines and, schedule permitting, catch a game. Dana and I joke over which of us owns more Cordova merchandise. He's our boy from when we were poor and loaning each other shirts so we didn't look like goofs at parties—so fuck the haters, we admire and praise his accomplishments.

In all the magazine articles and newspaper profiles, and I've read every one, the writers rehash the same crap on Dana: he travels on a private jet, drives a Ferrari, texts on an antiquated flip phone, loves blackjack—but there's no truer reflection of a man than his lifelong friends. It's a testament to Dana's character that he remains close with so many of us.

Question 3: What Do You Guys Do for Fun?

New York, Canada, Mexico, Brazil, Atlanta, New Orleans, Los Angeles—in every city and every country, the goal is let loose, eat and drink, and blow off steam. But the most anticipated destination is hardly the most luxurious: Levant, Maine, the small country town in which Dana spent his early childhood.

Soon as he made money he purchased a large tract that included his grandmother's drafty trailer. The strained relationship with both his mother and father is so overexposed in the media, but don't think Dana was some unloved orphan. For years he lived with his grandmother, a rock throw from cousins, aunts and uncles. And while walking those fields, the fresh air and tree-lined horizon, it's clear that during the drudgery and endless UFC meetings, this is where his mind wanders.

Environment shapes us, uplifts and breaks us. Since the first humans traversed the plains of Africa, more than parents and friends, environment molds. Overcrowded cities breed violence. Sweltering deserts, agitation. Wide forests, calm.

"Across that field—" Dana pointed to a trail vanishing into the trees "—when I was a kid my uncle bought me a horse. I thought it was cruel to cinch the saddle, so I'd ride her bareback through this field.

"And one day, she must've seen a snake because she bucked and threw me. Next thing I know, my head snaps and the lights go out. Kenny and David [cousins] freaked out, thought I was dead. They carried me back to the trailer, and my grandma held me all night, keeping me awake because we didn't have money for the doctor, so—"

So that's why Levant is home.

Later that night we walked those same moonlit fields, grass crunching underfoot. "This silence is what I dig most," he said. "The world is so fucking chaotic, but up here it's peaceful."

Question 4: How Does a Guy from a Broken Home, Who Barely Graduated High School, Never Completed Even a Semester of College, Come to Rule an Entire Industry?

Dana is the most successful fight promoter to ever walk the earth. There's really no debate—events promoted, cumulative tickets sold, broadcasts aired, fighters groomed—by virtually every empirical metric he's eclipsed Tex Rickard, Don King, Bob Arum.

Oh, how he despises the boxing promoters that have sucked the life from his first love. Every time we watch a PPV boxing match, and, yes, we catch every big fight, invariably there's Dana's pacing in front of the TV, bemoaning boxing's demise. "Those greedy motherfuckers. [Bob] Arum could have saved boxing, but all these years the pig hasn't invested a dollar in the sport."

What he means is: Bob Arum and Don King take their cut of the purse and run, vanishing until the next bout. Here's all it takes to promote boxing (hypothetical example): Get two boxers to agree on a bout for $1 million each. Next, call HBO and say, "I've got these boxers matched up, how much will you pay me? Six million? Okay." Now call MGM Casino and tell those guys, "I've got HBO and these two boxers, you keep the gate, we'll split the merchandise sales, how much will you pay me? Seven million? Okay . . ." The fight happens, and afterward everyone counts their money, and the promoters vanish until the next bout. "All you need to promote boxing is a secretary and a fax machine," Dana says.

On the flipside, the UFC "four walls" the event—which means they handle everything: broadcast production, ticket and merchandise sales, designing posters, you name it. The organization 24/7 promotes its fighters, pushes them in the *UFC* magazine and *The Ultimate Fighter*, features them on the UFC website, the television shows, video blogs, billboards. Drive down the highway, enter a grocery store, flip on the TV, wherever you turn it's UFC Nation. And because they do everything and control everything, they deliver product that eclipses boxing.

So there's good reason for Dana to ask, Where the FUCK is the boxing equivalent?!

Now you can appreciate what he's really accomplished. Not even P.T. Barnum rescued a floundering industry. Oh, and let's not skip his ancillary credits: television producer, merchandising exec, marketing maven, Twitter maestro, YouTube star, and so on.

Now I don't want to get all glum here, but to ignore Dana's upbringing is to ignore a major component of his makeup. I'm talking childhood. The foundation that provides us with confidence, stability, and a healthy self-image. In short, Dana's father was a violent alcoholic, often absent for months at a time. And his mother, well, I'll let Dana's sister, Kelly, recount life in the White household: "'You're going to be a fucking loser, just like your father,' our mother

Dana White, holding court at the Beacon Theater, NYC.

used to tell Dana, 'You know all your rich friends at school? Well, you're going to be pumping their gas.'"

So again: how does a kid, barely graduating high school, acquire a bankrupt company and turn around not only that entity but also an entire sport?

Read enough business bios and you'll appreciate the two ingredients in every success: (1) relentless hustle and sacrifice and (2) a model for that success.

HUSTLE AND SACRIFICE

At nineteen, while manning the bell desk at the Boston Harbor hotel, Dana decided to start boxing, so he sought out Peter Welch, a former Golden Gloves champ and legendary trainer in South Boston. "If I was going to box, I wanted to learn from the best," Dana said, "and what's crazy is, though everyone knew the guy, he was so mysterious and elusive it took me months of asking around, dropping by gyms, before I tracked him down."

He put in the hours with Welch. Which meant training to box, really box, not just get in shape. Hours on the mitts, the bags, knocked senseless while sparring. After a few months in this new environment, he looked around and realized he wanted to do this every day of his life—which beat schlepping suitcases, hauling gravel, anything he'd done before. So he partnered with Peter, and they started signing clients. At the time, traditional gyms catered only to core boxers. That's just how it was. But Peter and Dana saw the opportunity and decided to train all comers.

They gave free lessons. Taught group sessions. Built the business until the business attracted unwanted attention from Whitey Bulger's crew, etc. etc.

Top: Lorenzo meeting with GSP after his Condit win.
Bottom: Dana on-stage for a fan Q&A.

This is well-trodden territory, so I'm going to detour from the known narrative and fill in a personal gap. What the magazines haven't reported is that while living in Boston, every few weeks he was on the phone with a girl. From Vegas. Who we'd grown up with, and who he'd crushed on since the day they met in eighth grade. So when Dana left Boston for Vegas, it was Anne Stella who picked him up at the airport, and they've been together ever since.

The morning after he landed, he nabbed a job parking cars at a local hospital. In the off-hours he visited local gyms, and damn if the boxing/aerobics craze hadn't yet arrived. No, he wasn't certified, as required by state regulations, and, no, he didn't have a client book to prove his worth as a trainer—but the nascent promoter talked a local gym owner into giving him a chance, so again he quit a job for boxing, and soon he was packing them in for the group sessions and became the biggest draw in the city.

Compressing these events into a convenient narrative in so many ways diminishes the struggle, the fear, and the sacrifice. Quitting a steady job after tying the knot, trying to launch a new business while friends and family scoff—unless you've entered that dark cave, it's hard to fathom. The fighter's journey without elbows to the face.

"Bro, on Sundays I'd spar a hundred rounds with clients," Dana told me. "Money got so tight, I didn't have a choice. I'd spar until the skin peeled off my feet. At the end of every five-week cycle I'd pocket three grand, which paid for groceries, diapers, formula. It was fucking rough."

Especially after Anne left her six-figure job at the Mirage Hotel & Casino in order to give birth to their first son, Dana White III. The next year, son Aidan. Dawn to dusk Dana taught privates and four nights a week group classes. "24 Hour Fitness paid me $150 a class. That was unheard of—usually it was $12 per, but I brought in so many students, other clubs wanted me."

Next, he hit on a strategy: in the gym business, overhead devours profit. It's the leash that keeps most owners on the floor, personally working with clients. But if he partnered with a wealthy client and opened a private gym, he could hire other trainers and free himself to open the next private gym. Rinse and repeat.

Which begs the question: how did he convince wealthy investors to back him in these ventures? Answer, the same way he garnered so many clients. In the groundbreaking book *Emotional Intelligence*, author Dan Goleman, a science reporter for the *New York Times*, probed the link between academic IQ and business success. To prove a point, Goleman profiled scientists at Bell Labs, the world-famous think tank where of course you'd rank high IQ as the leading asset. But the results startled even him, for it wasn't the most academically gifted that rose to leadership positions but researchers that excelled in conflict resolution, self-motivation, and communicating empathy. In summary: Across every field, whether bio-tech or construction, great leaders possess the highest degrees of emotional intelligence. And if there's one thing I can say about Dana, he is, and always has been, a social animal.

Despite a lack of formal education, Dana is also one of the most intellectually curious people I know. For days on end we hole up in his movie room and watch political documentaries. While traveling, we tour historical sites. "School bored the fuck out of me." He laughed. "But riding my bike around Boston, I'd listen to audio tapes on marketing, business strategy, motivational talks. Anything to teach me about success. Every night I'd fall asleep with headphones playing."

"It's crazy, coming from someone who didn't last a week in college, but education is critical. Not school, but real knowledge. You've got to learn everything you can about the industry you want to enter, from every means at your disposal. Work in the mailroom. Sweep the floors. Talk to people. Intern. Read. And most important, don't ever quit, no matter how many roadblocks you hit, because you will hit roadblocks. That's just the nature of life. I can't tell you how many people have told me no."

During all this Dana trained a handful of amateur and pro boxers, but the constant hassles wear on him. Boxers never keep their word. Never pay commissions on time.

They are, quite simply, a difficult bunch. So the fight business loses its luster, until he meets John Lewis, a UFC fighter. Together they attend a few MMA events. Dana interacts with the tribe, and this rekindles his love for the fight game. "MMA fighters are a different breed from boxers. You've got to realize, boxing programs rescue troubled kids from inner-city streets, but martial arts schools exist in middle-class neighborhoods. The parents are involved. The kids work hard in school. Same with wrestlers, most go to college. It's just a different world."

Around this time, at a mutual friend's wedding, Dana reconnected with Lorenzo Fertitta. Which now seems fated: Dana teaching boxing, Lorenzo serving as a commissioner on the Nevada State Athletic Commission. Lorenzo wanted to get in shape, so he dropped by Dana's gym. Big brother Frank joined the workouts, and the three grew close.

Very close.

BUSINESS LINEAGE

In 1993, Lorenzo left New York University armed with an MBA and a desire to make his mark. In the mid- to late 1990s, as the tech world heated up, he ran a venture fund from what is now the UFC headquarters. There he'd pour over investment proposals, listen to pitches, monitor the family portfolio. Since the 1980s he'd served as director of the publicly traded Station Casinos, the enterprise started by his father, Frank Fertitta, Jr., so he knew the long game: scour business opportunities for an underexploited niche, invest in the company, nurture it through the rough times, then reap.

This timeworn strategy under-girds our capitalist system. Thomas Edison, Henry Ford, Steve Jobs—each legendary entrepreneur enticed an investor to fund his vision.

Top: Dana, in Levant, Maine.
Bottom: Marty Cordova, Dana, and Nick backstage.

The UFC wasn't Lorenzo's first rodeo. In 1995, he invested in Gordon Biersch, and stepping in as president and CEO he oversaw the rapid expansion of distribution and also the growth and sale of the company's restaurant division. Then, from 1997 to 1999, he helped friends Timothy Poster and Tom Breitling launch Travelscape, a company that provided room reservations at Las Vegas hotels. From a back office at the Palace Station casino they grew the business, migrating from telemarketing phone banks to the Internet, and in early 2000 they sold the company to Expedia (parent company, Microsoft) for a hefty chunk.

In 1996, Lorenzo joined the Nevada State Athletic Commission as a commissioner. Growing up he watched boxing with his father and brother and, of course, like any kid in the 1970s, idolized Muhammad Ali. So when he began training with Dana, that steady *clack-clack-clack* wasn't just the speed bag ricocheting off the platform, it was the invisible gears in motion.

To facilitate workouts, Lorenzo built a private gym in his office building's basement. He tapped Dana to design the gym, then allowed him to train clients there for free in exchange for helping run the facility. Now take note, for this right here is the lucky break of Dana's career. Not moving back to Vegas, or chancing into Lorenzo at the wedding, or even the famed Griffin versus Bonnar bout. Or the Fox deal. No, it was the arrangement with this private gym. So you're telling me that a deal involving a tiny weight room for some millionaire prepared Dana White to conquer the corporate world?

Yes. Because the gym's proximity to Lorenzo's M&A activities provided an unobstructed view of the process by which companies are launched. There is no success in a vacuum. Much as we think ourselves so smart, so creative, so original—that's just the little reels looping in our heads.

Dana addresses Nike conference.

During the 1970s, Japanese researchers documented macaque monkeys on the island of Koshima washing potatoes in a river, which was odd. Where the hell'd they learned that? But even crazier was how the younger monkeys watched, and mimicked, and before long twenty monkeys stood in the river, scrubbing away. New Age gurus embellished and repackaged the anecdote as a lesson in sweeping ideological change, the "100th Monkey Effect"—but there's another message: to truly understand any behavior, find its model.

So here I am, scouring every article on the rise of UFC, and they're all the same: a few photos, a few direct quotes, a few well-worn milestones—the "chance reunion of Dana and Lorenzo at a friend's wedding," the Zuffa acquisition, the financial hardships, *The Ultimate Fighter* success, the Fox Network deal; but not one write-up explained how a guy with zero corporate experience lifted an entire sport from the ashes and into the national consciousness, in the process trouncing such business titans as Donald Trump, Mark Cuban, and Viacom.

What, where, when doesn't always answer how. But it's not that complicated a riddle, once you consider those monkeys. Or, as this is a book on MMA, let's return to the dojo, where every great jiu-jitsu practitioner is first and foremost evaluated via lineage. Take Royce's pedigree:

Mitsuyo Maeda > Carlos Gracie > Helio Gracie > Royce Gracie

Business is no different. Information and practices flow mentor to student, each sensei modeling success and imparting wisdom. Neither Steve Jobs nor Bill Gates graduated college, but they both learned from mentors—for Jobs, Robert Noyce; for Gates, Dr. Ed Roberts.

So here's Dana's business lineage:

Mr. Frank Fertitta, Jr. > Frank Fertitta III > Lorenzo Fertitta > Dana White

Mr. Frank Fertitta, Jr. founded Station Casinos in the mid-seventies, and after taking the company public in 1993, he retired and son Frank stepped in as president.

To say Mr. Fertitta mentored his sons is an understatement. "From a young age he exposed Frank and Lorenzo to every aspect of the company," Dana told me. "He loved to talk business with them. It's how they bonded."

For years D.W. watched Lorenzo work, quietly attending meetings, listening to investment details over lunches/dinners, so when he learned the UFC was on the blocks, he thought, This is it, the opportunity every investor seeks. . . if I pitch this correctly, we could really grow this thing and bring it from the Dark Ages . . . I could get into the fight business like I always wanted.

"What's crazy is that a month before this I was approached by an investor who was launching the WFA [World Fighting Alliance, a rival MMA organization] and they guy offered me a car, a house, and a good salary, to run the thing," Dana told me, "This was a great deal, but when I told Lorenzo, he looked at me like, 'Are you fucking serious, I thought we were going to do something together.' I said, 'Done, I'm not doing it.'"

Was that difficult to turn down?

"No, if I was going into business with someone, I wanted it to be Lorenzo. I just didn't know if he was serious. I mean, he's got a lot going on. And the question becomes, what are we going to do, promote boxing? We'd have to start from scratch—which of course we would have figured out—but there was nothing on the table. Then, not even a month later, I find out the UFC is in trouble and for sale. I call him up and go dude—'

Although Royce never trained with the long-deceased Maeda, following the UFC acquisition, Dana established his personal war-room adjacent to Mr. Fertitta's office. Every afternoon the two met, sensei and student.

"He didn't approve of their investing in the company, and this was a big deal, as they had never gone against his advice. But thankfully, this time they went with their guts and bought the thing, and what's amazing is Mr. Fertitta never held it against me. Every afternoon he'd come in and we'd discuss marketing, the books, even fighter negotiations. I learned from him, and in turn he learned about the fight business, which allowed him to continue those discussions with his boys."

For me, the question is, why invest with Dana? The Fertitta brothers have plenty of friends. Highly educated friends. And on paper, the brothers couldn't appear more different from Dana—they come from stable families, he doesn't. They come from money, he doesn't. They were both educated at elite universities, he wasn't.

But they share something more important than biographical stats. They share a ruthless competitive ethos. "It's just how I see the world," Dana told me, "when you get up every morning life is ready to kick you in the face, and you better be ready to kick back."

Is this due to your dysfunctional home life?

"Listen, I like to win. I don't know why, but I am a fucking conqueror. And it's not just Affliction, Pride, or Viacom [competing organizations]. When we go live on Saturday night, I want to beat the NBA. I want to beat the NFL. Come Monday I can't wait to check the ratings. This last weekend in Winnipeg, the biggest gate they'd ever done was $1.8 million, set by the Rolling Stones. We did $3.2 million. We smashed the Rolling Stones. That pumps me more than anything. I always want to win. That's what fuels me."

That motivates you more than the curse? I say, and we both laugh. Around the corporate offices there's talk of a "UFC curse"—as in all that defy the UFC, sooner or later, lose; whether it's a competing brand, a disloyal employee, or a seditious fighter. And Dana loves to watch them fall.

"Yeah, I can hold a grudge. When I used to go out and try and sell the UFC, I'd have doors slammed in my face so fast, and yes, that drove me harder. I'd think, You'll see, motherfucker, you're going to want this someday, and I'm not going to forget it. Take DC shoes. I used to love that brand. I wore the shirts, the shoes, you name it. I mean, skateboarding is like the biggest renegade sport in the world—for years everybody shit on skateboarders. So one day I call them and tell them their logo would look great

in the Octagon, and they said they would never, *ever* be involved in a sport like that. I'm not kidding you when I tell you that night I went home and burned every fucking DC thing I owned. To this day I won't wear DC. I love Rob Dyrdek, but I wouldn't even buy DC for my kids."

That's it: whether fueled by dreams of conquering the world or simple vengeance, Dana is the most driven person I know. I crash and he's still on the phone. I wake and he's pacing the room. Slow down, relax, I tell him, but he just scoffs. If you're looking for a roadmap, that's how the most "unlikely to succeed" conquers all.

Two years ago I followed Dana into that arena. The lights. The noise. The energy. As a friend, I needed to understand this world. So I dove down the rabbit hole, and you're holding the result. Here's my take-away:

MMA is the most misunderstood sport on the planet. On talk shows and news reports, critics wag fingers and complain that hand-to-hand combat somehow undermines society—but their arguments ignore how this "mock combat" unites and inspires us. Whether it's reality-as-theater or theater-as-reality, the hero's journey transcends borders, languages, and cultures; and for the fighters, the cage is the field upon which they test their resolve.

Dana's story isn't simply one of wealth or fame; it's the story of a disadvantaged kid who took on the world and won. It's the story of a fighter.

14: FIGHT WEEK

1. Build it and they will come—arena construction.
2. Brock Lesnar and Alistair Overeem selling the fight.
3. Pre-fight Thursday press conference—Seattle, Washington, December 2012.
4. Friday: Backstage of the official weigh-in: Fighters await their call. Here Dana talks with Diaz camp.
5. One by one the fighters take the stage, weigh in, then face off for the cameras. Here Brad Pickett versus Eddie Wineland.
6. After weigh-ins fighters gather for "Fighter Speech," in which Dana inspires the fighters and offers performances bonuses.
7. Always amped! Clay Guida, post weigh-in, ready to eat.
8. Fighter bus, on the way back to the hotel. Here: T.J. Dillashaw and Justin Buchholz.
9. Friday night: Dana approves every walkout song.
10. Craig Borsari heads up production meeting.
11. Fans run for free tickets announced via Twitter.
12. Skipper Kelp hands out free tickets.
13. Nick the Tooth and Joe Lauzon grappling for *UFC 155* video blog.
14. Nick and Dana at Temple Bar, Dublin, Ireland.
15. Nick the Tooth and Brad Pickett filming. London, England.
16. Nick the Tooth quenches his thirst. Levant, Maine.
17. Fight Night.
18. Cageside seats; the monitor is often the best view.
19. "Making the Rounds": Arianny Celeste.
20. "Best Seat in the House": Brittney Palmer.
21. Victory: Matt Brown. *UFC on Fox: Henderson versus Diaz.*

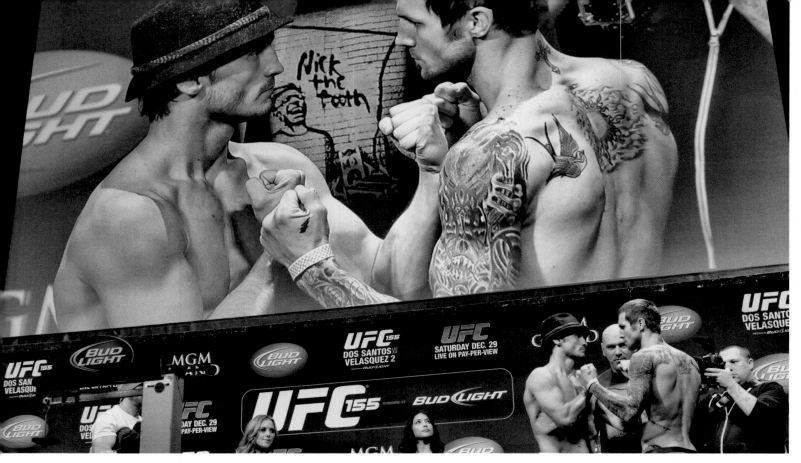

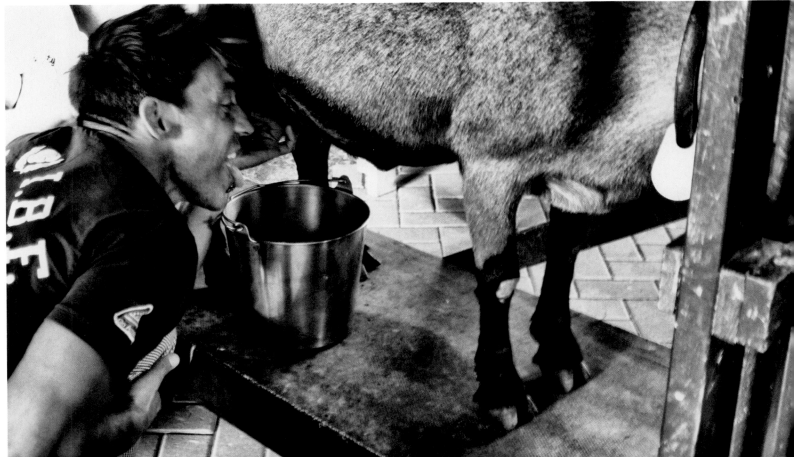

PHOTOGRAPHIC CAPTIONS AND CREDITS

Pages vi-vii: Joel Kinnaman, star of *Robocop*, enters the arena.

Chapter 1: Into the cage, Ken Stone.

Chapter 2: Dana White and Royce Gracie, talking cageside.

Chapter 3: Rory MacDonald training.

Chapter 4: Chad Mendes emerges victorious.

Chapter 5: The Tao of Silva: Anderson backstage with Rodrigo Damm.

Chapter 6: B.J. Penn vs. Rory MacDonald.

Chapter 7: Myles Jury surfing.

Chapter 8: Jon Jones.

Chapter 9: Ronda Rousey, the first UFC Women's Champion

Chapter 10: Cast members look at *The Ultimate Fighter* wall of fame.

Chapter 11: *UFC 148*.

Chapter 12: Joe Rogan calling the fight.

Chapter 13: Dana White.

Chapter 14: Weigh-in in New Orleans.

Additional image credits: page 22, designed by Roots of Fight, images courtesy of UFC; page 28, designed by Roots of Fight, image courtesy of Shannon Lee and Bruce Lee Enterprises, www.brucelee.com; page 30, designed by Roots of Fight, images courtesy of The Gracie Academy.

ACKNOWLEDGMENTS

Taylor and Carson, my two girls: for your unending support, and sharing this ride.

Dana White: for a lifelong friendship, and always letting me be me.

Lorenzo and Frank Fertitta: for your patience and generosity.

Anne and the kids: for sharing your home and always laughing at the madness.

The entire UFC tribe—the staff, the fighters, the managers—too many to name, but a few that went beyond the call of duty: Craig Borsari, Kirk Hendrick, Rich Chou, Ed Soares, Jesse Katz, Joe Rogan, Reed Harris, Fredson Paixao, Joe Williams, Isabelle Hodges, Donna Marcolini, Dave Sholler.

Pat Tenore: for supporting artists.

My early readers: Jeremy Asher Lynch, my brother Tony.

David Forrer, my agent: for pushing this project when the odds were long.

Jenny Bradshaw: the most patient and generous editor an author could want.

Jordan Fenn, Leah Springate, Janine Laporte, and Ruta Liormonas: for publishing, designing, producing, and spreading the word about the book.

My parents: for putting that first book in my hands.